TWENTIETH CENTURY
WWI Reenvisioned Twenty

GARY LEE KVAMME

Volume 27

Telling Art Series

Copyright © 2017 by Gary Lee Kvamme

All rights reserved.

Published September 2017

TWENTIETH CENTURY
WWI Reenvisioned Twenty

A new array of paintings combining loose, freewheeling brushwork with a minimal palette of colors to convey the vast and varied aspects of the First World War.

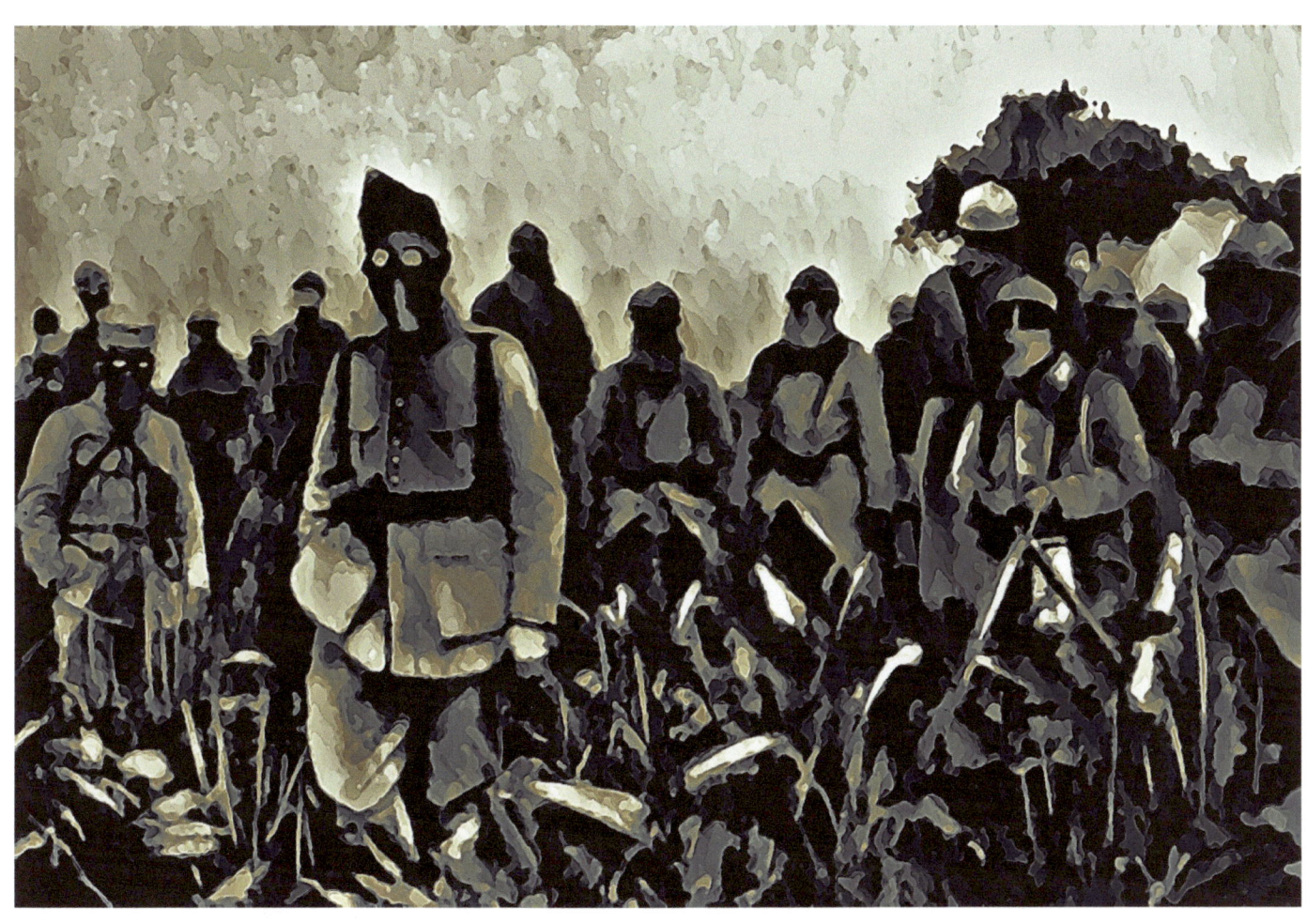
HAVING RECEIVED WARNING THAT GAS WAS BEING DISCHARGED AGAINST THEM, THE FRENCH SOLDIERS MASKED THEMSELVES SECURELY AGAINST THE DEADLY FUMES AND AWAITED THE THREATENED ATTACK WITH CONFIDENCE.

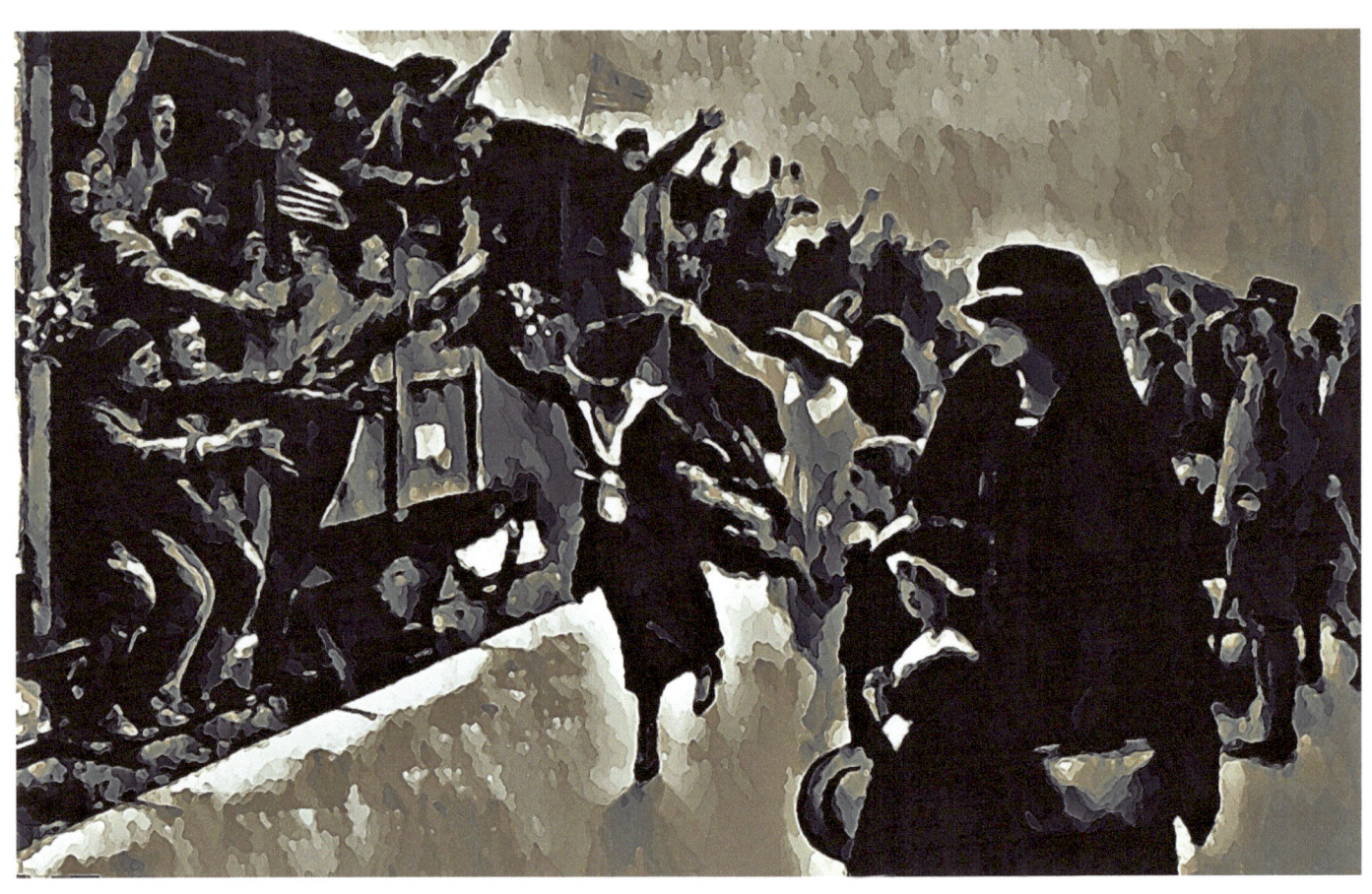

TROOP TRAIN PASSING THROUGH A PARIS SUBURBAN STATION CARRYING ENTHUSIASTIC AMERICAN SOLDIERS TO THE WESTERN FRONT.

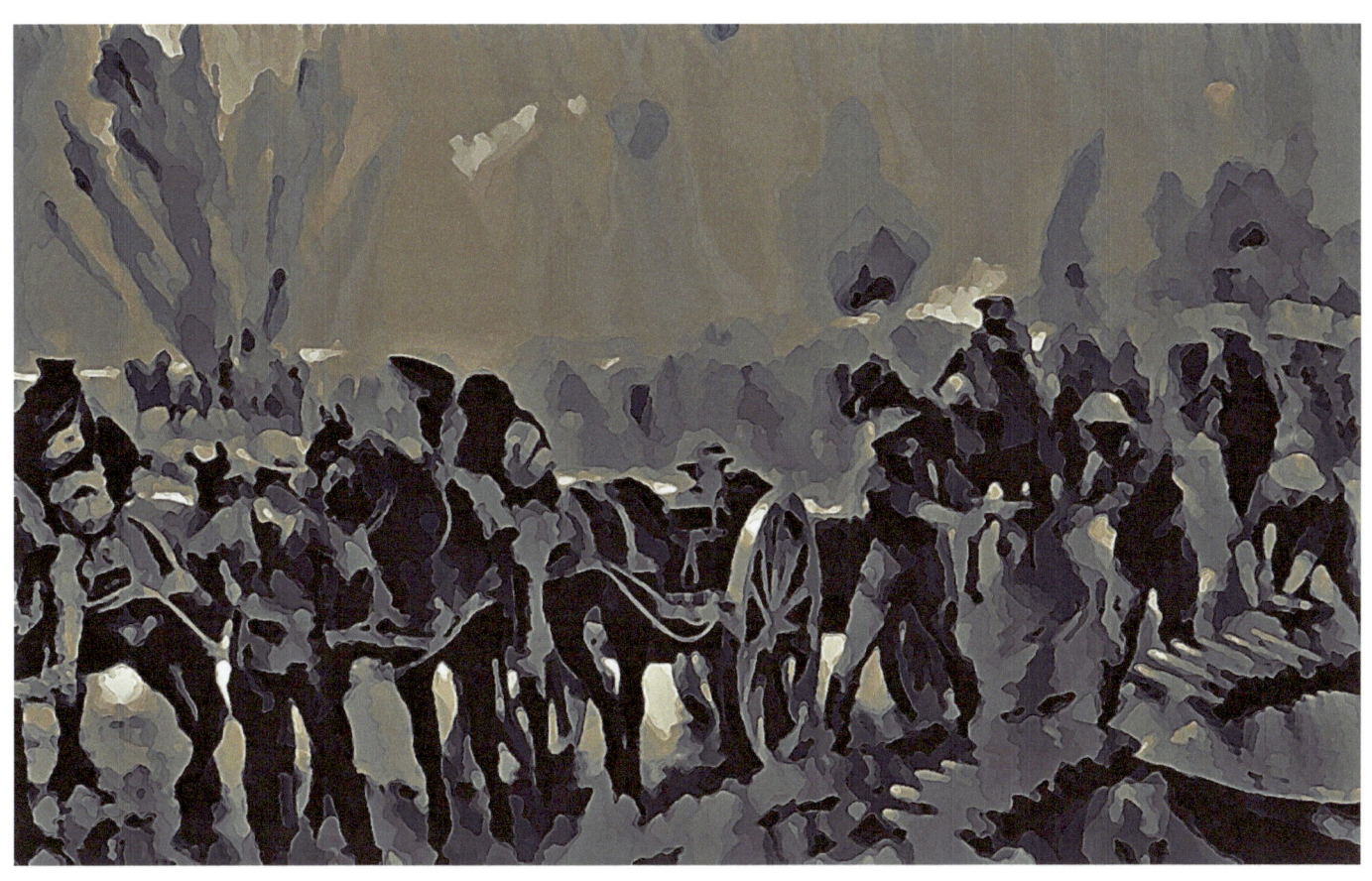

WHILE AN ATTACK IS TAKING PLACE THE ADVANCED FIELD-GUNS NEVER CEASE FIRING, AND AN ENDLESS CHAIN OF WAGONS BRINGS UP AMMUNITION TO THE DUMPS CLOSE TO THE GUN-PITS.

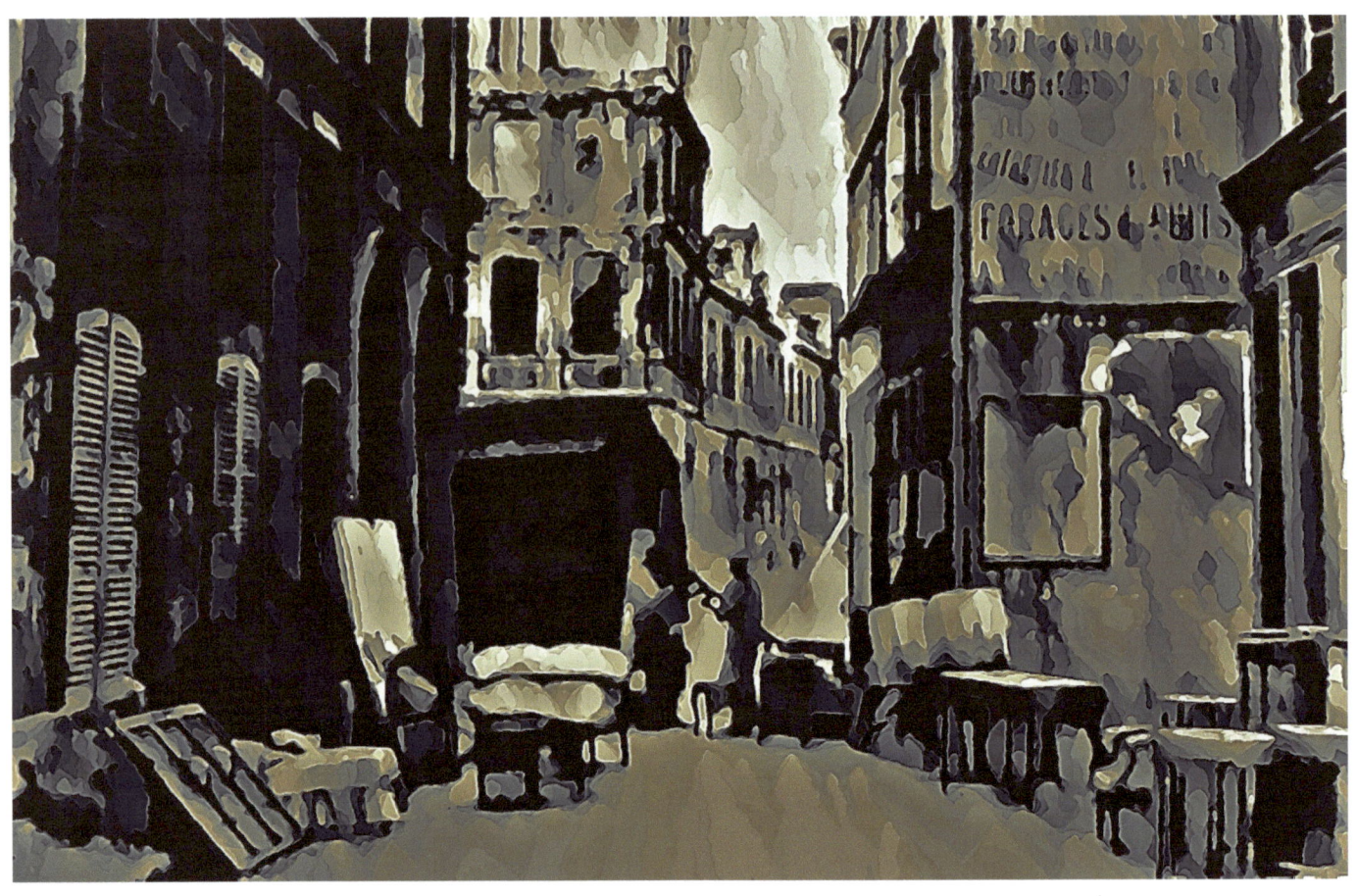

"HOUSEHOLD REMOVAL" DURING BOMBARDMENT—A SCENE IN ONE OF THE STREETS OF MUCH-STRICKEN RHEIMS. THOUGH THE ANCIENT CITY SUFFERED TERRIBLE DEVASTATION MANY OF THE INHABITANTS LONG REFUSED TO LEAVE, AND WHEN THEY AT LENGTH DECIDED TO DO SO THE REMOVAL WAS CARRIED OUT IN UNHASTING FASHION.

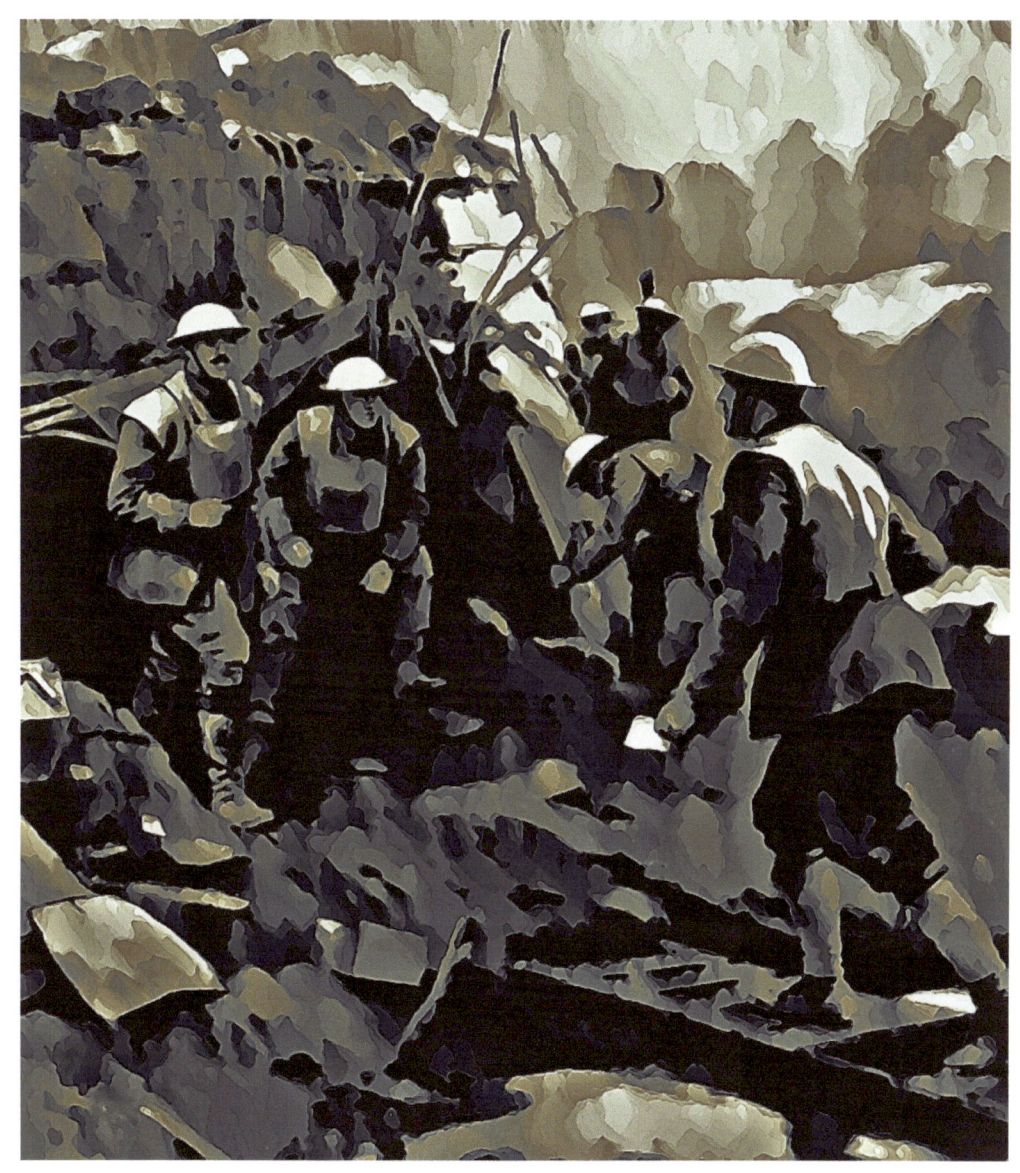

NEWS OF BATTLE FROM THE FIRING-LINE.

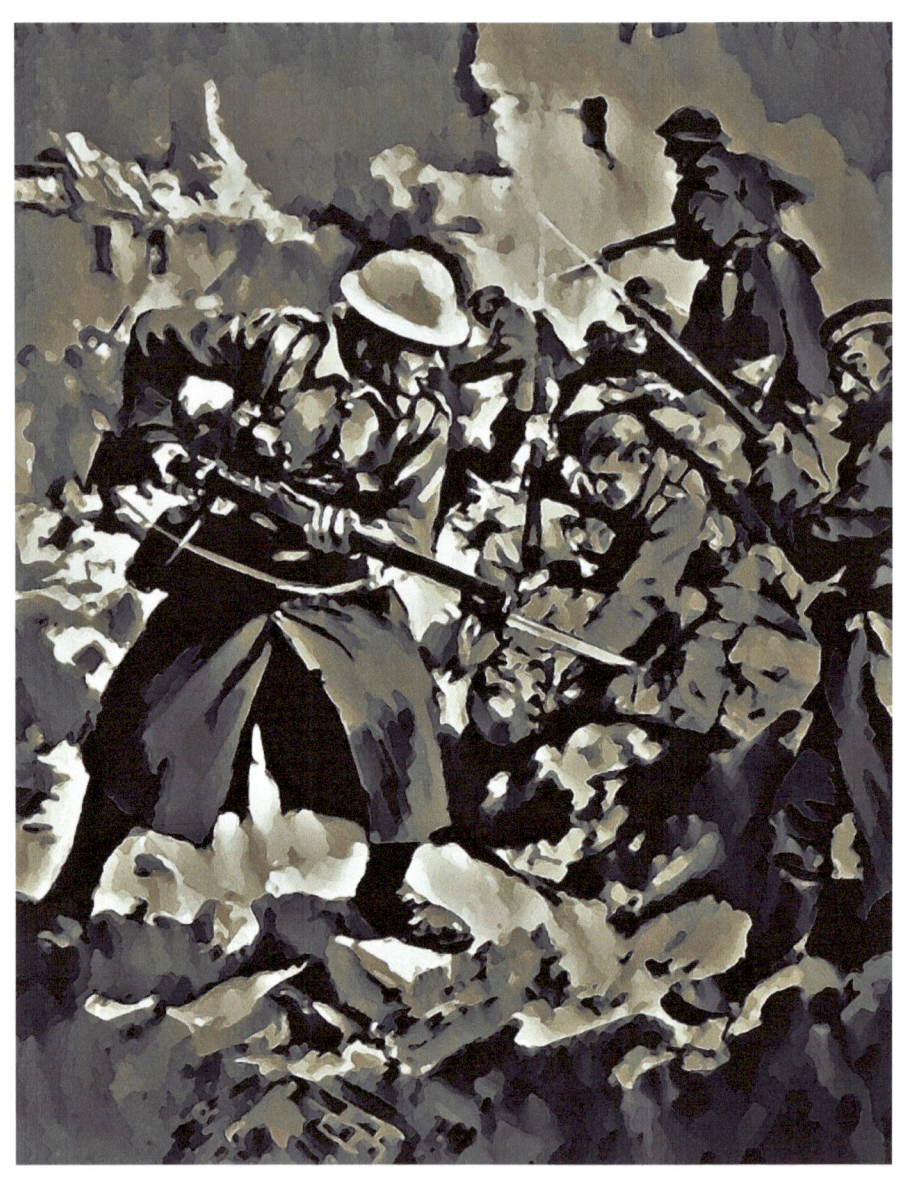

MAN-HUNTING AMID THE SHATTERED WALLS OF PUISIEUX.

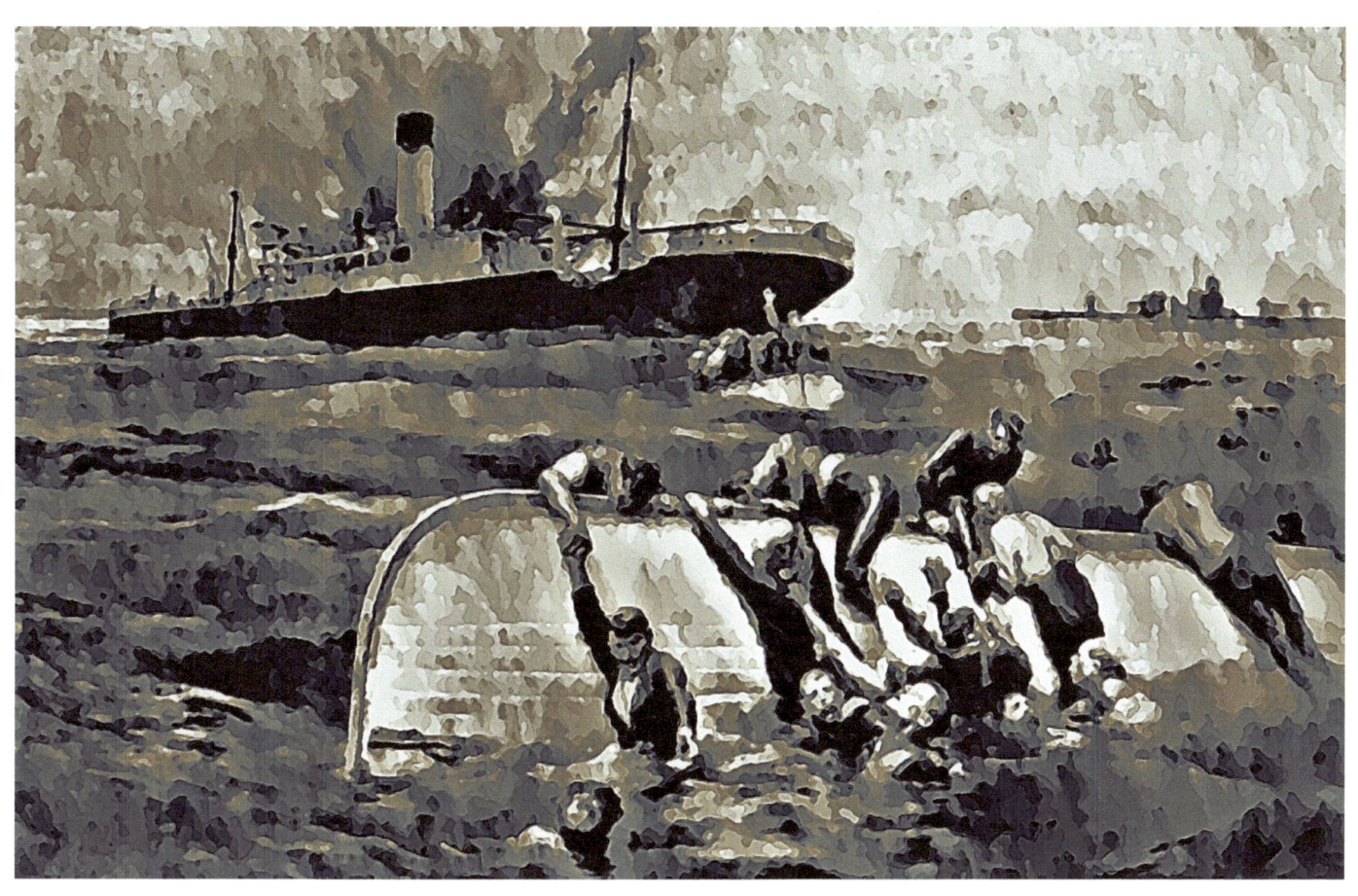

FIRED ON WITHOUT WARNING, THE DIOMED WAS SUNK WEST OF THE SCILLY ISLES. BOATS WERE HURRIEDLY LAUNCHED, BUT ONE CAPSIZED, AND MANY OF THE CREW WERE DROWNED.

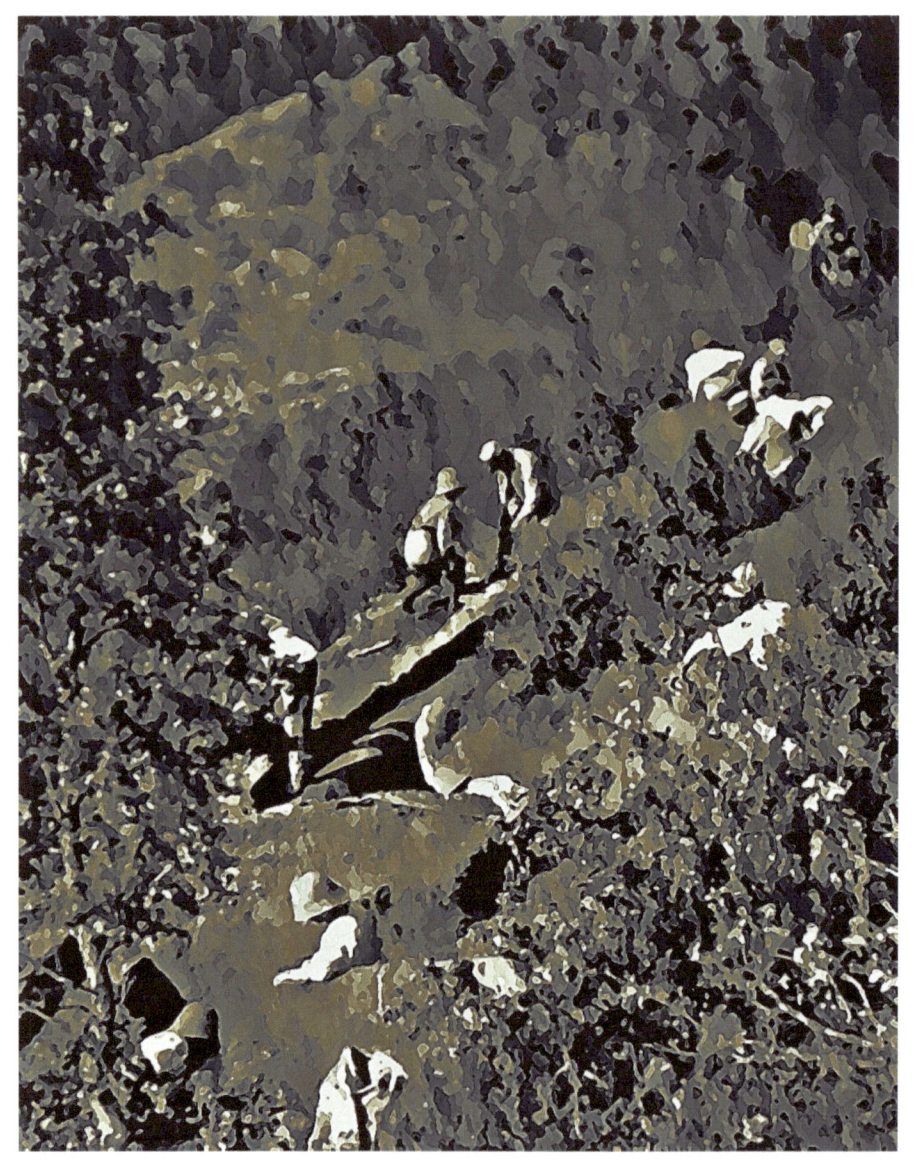

ENTRENCHING IN THE HILLS NEAR MONASTIR.

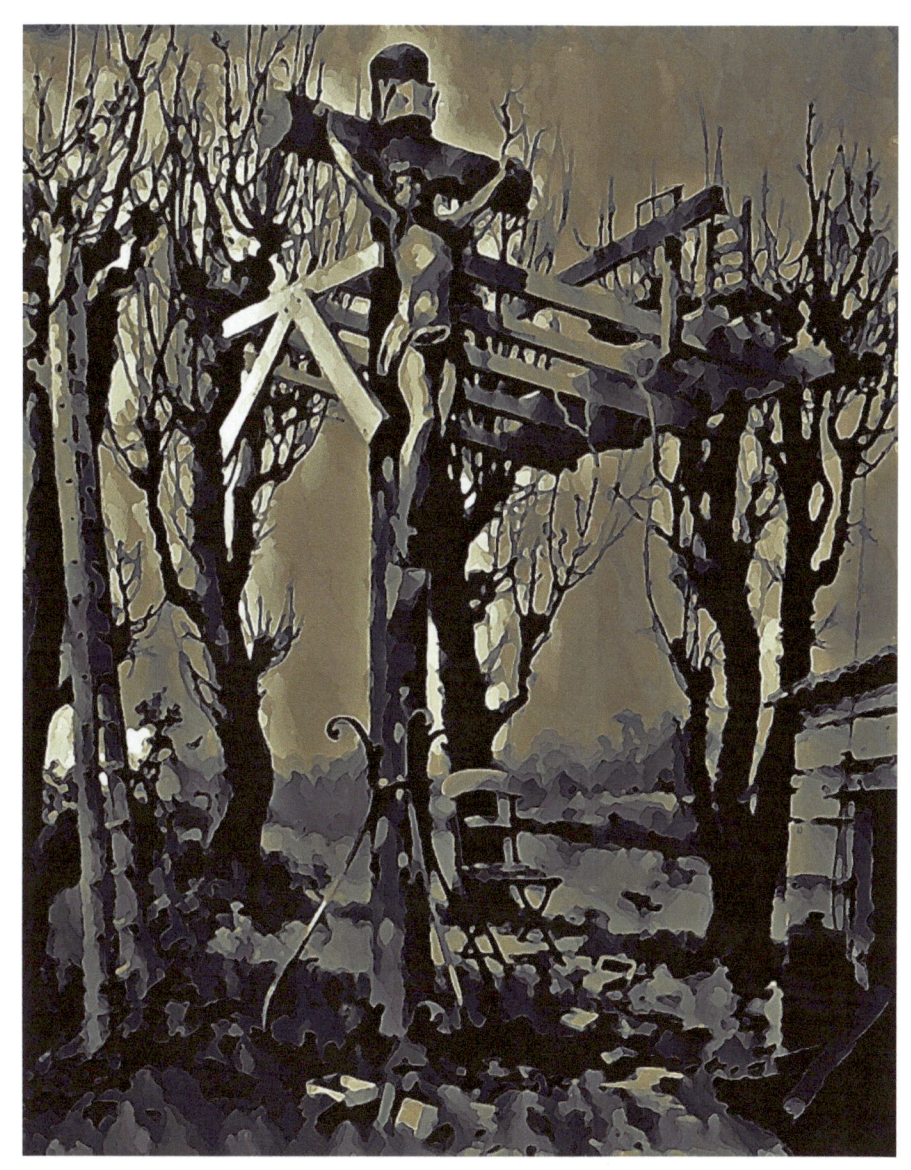

APPALLING GERMAN ABUSE OF WAYSIDE CALVARY.

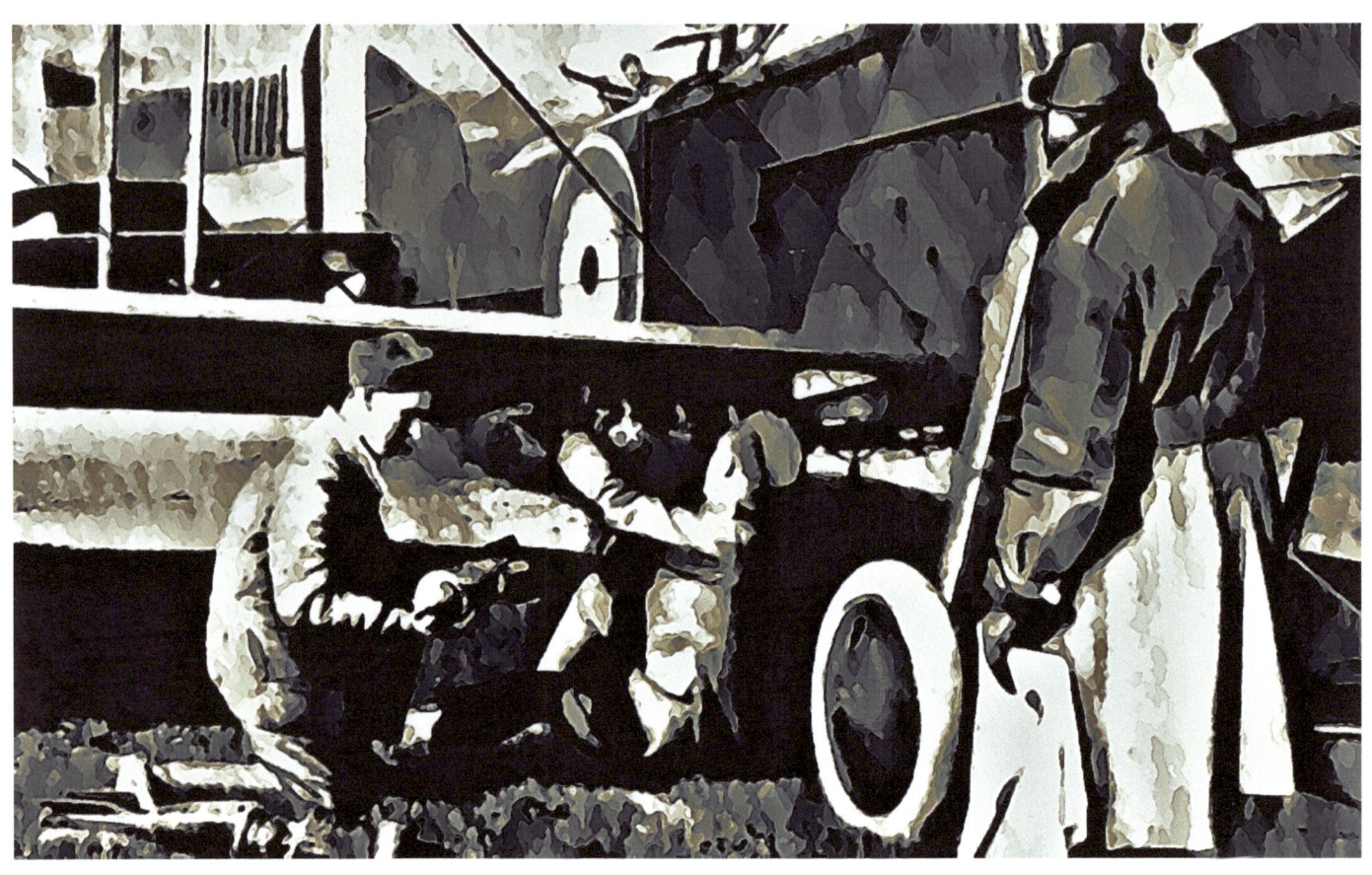
BRITISH AERIAL ACTIVITY ON THE WESTERN FRONT. FIXING BOMBS TO DROP ON MASSED GERMANS.

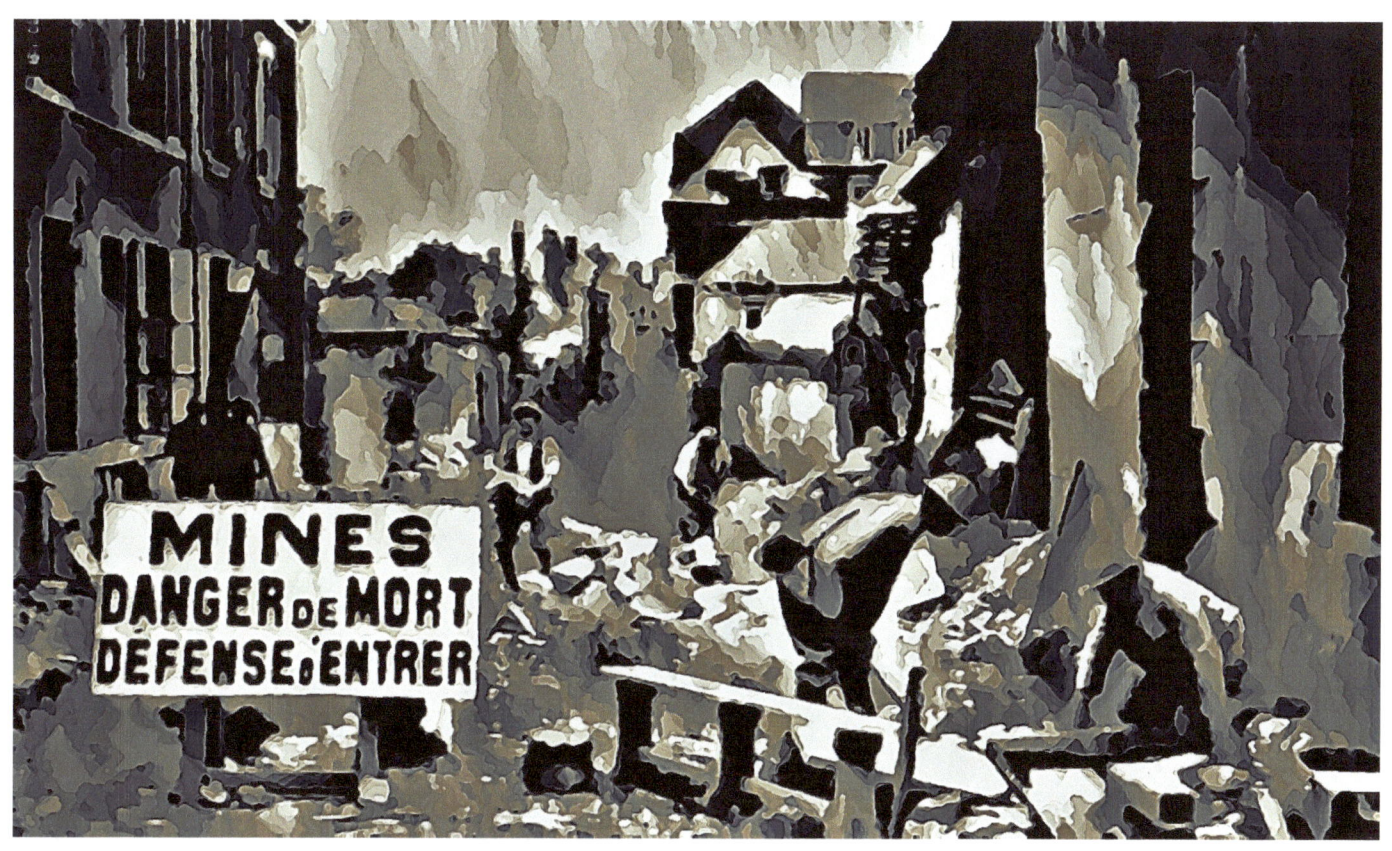
FRENCH ENGINEERS SEARCHING THE STREETS OF NOYON FOR MINES LAID BY THE GERMANS WHEN EVACUATING THE TOWN.

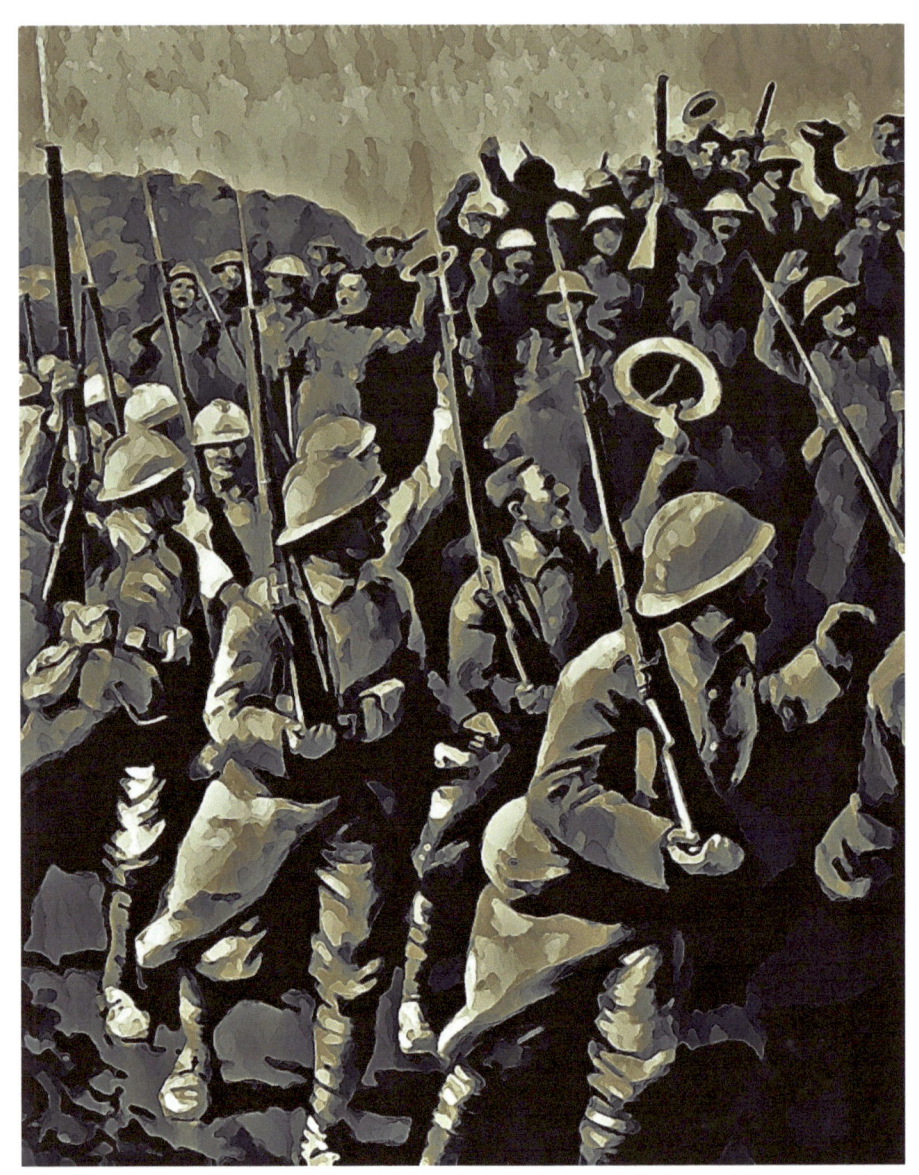
CHANGING GUARD SOMEWHERE ON THE SOMME.

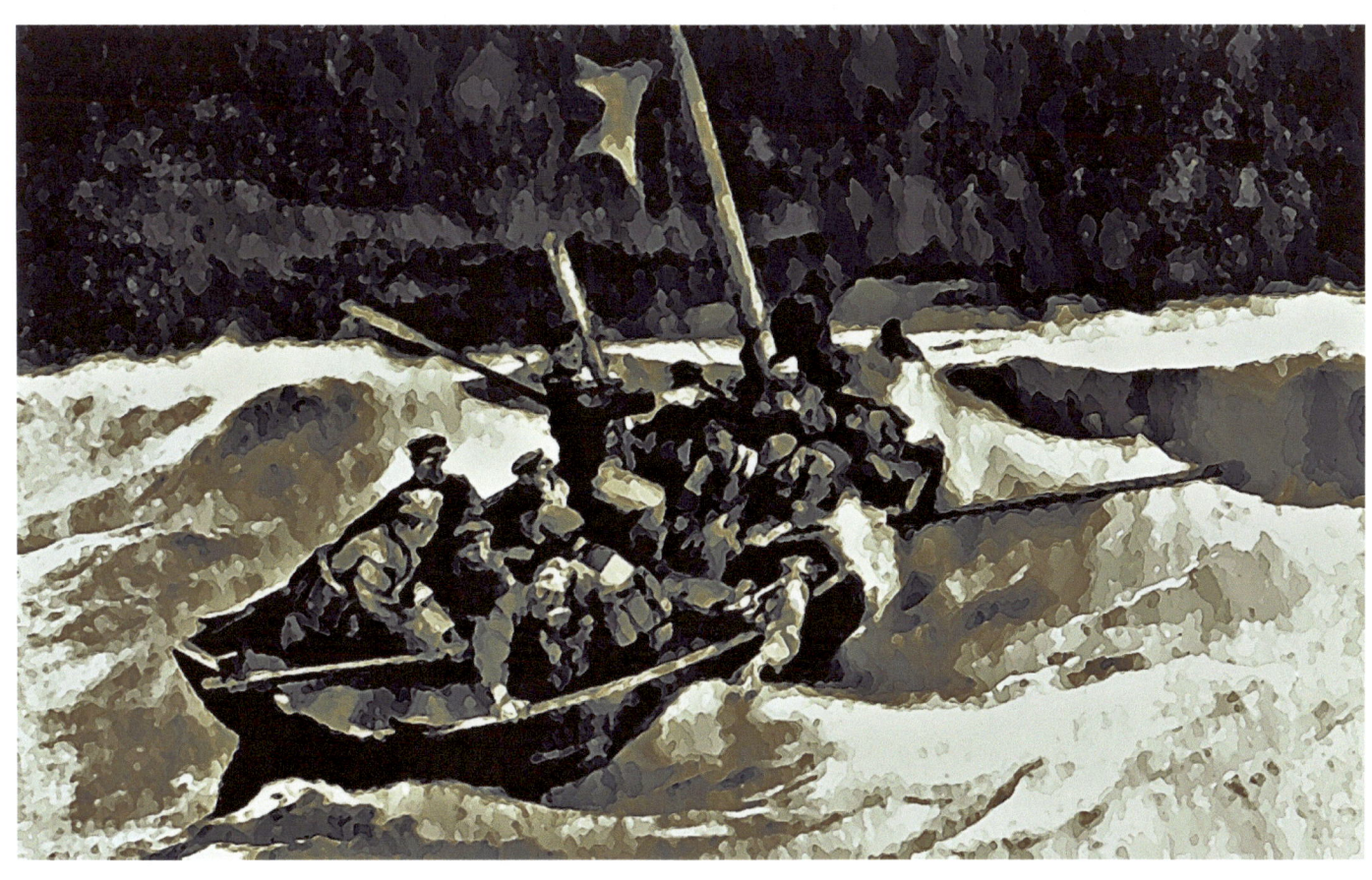

MEN OF THE LIVERPOOL STEAMER ARTIST, TORPEDOED BY A GERMAN U-BOAT IN A WINTRY GALE.

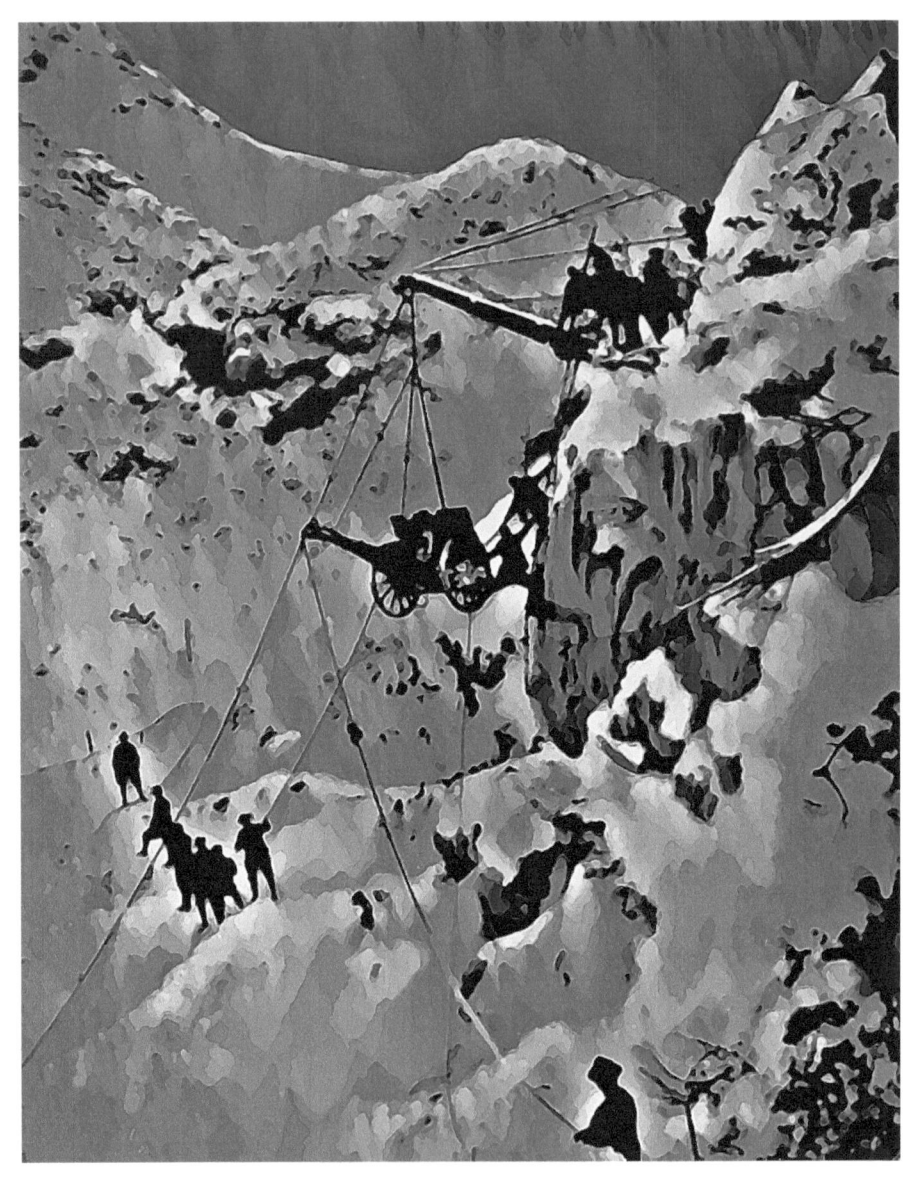

GREAT GUNS TO THE FIRING-LINE BY POWERFUL CRANE.

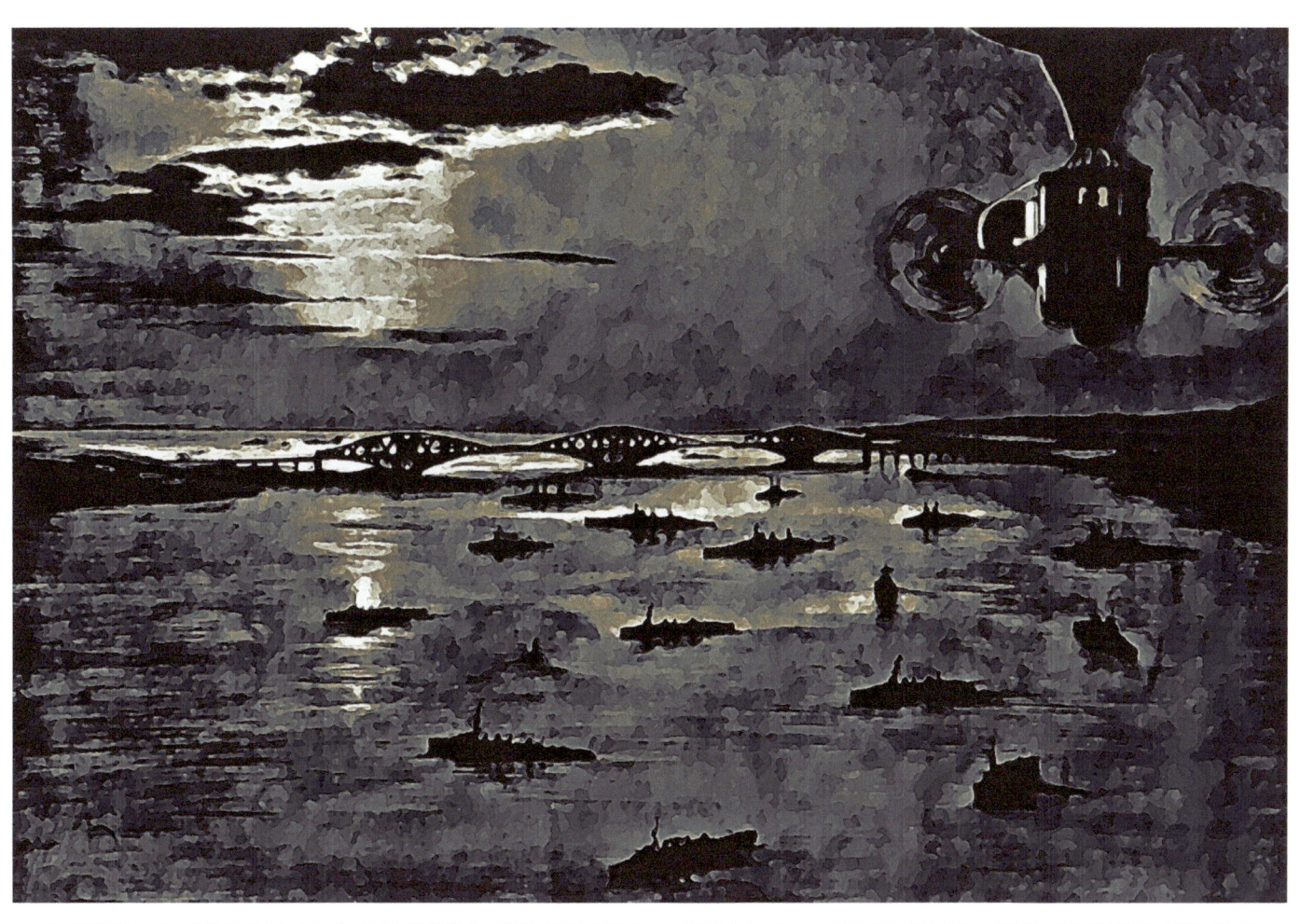

BRITAIN'S NAVAL MIGHT: CRUISER SQUADRONS LYING OFF ROSYTH, IN THE FIRTH OF FORTH.

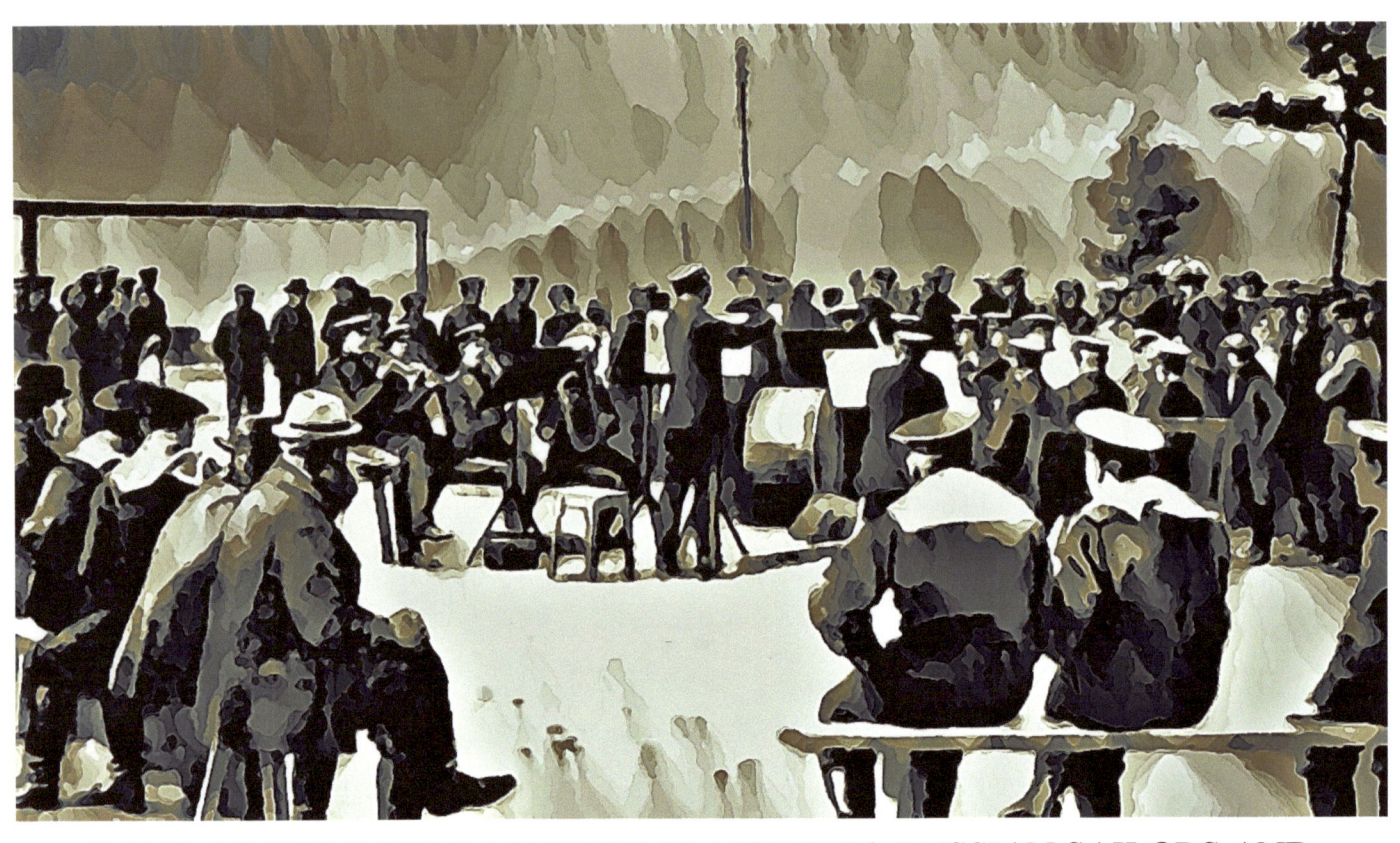
BAND OF THE ROYAL MARINES PLAYING TO RUSSIAN SAILORS AND WORKMEN SOMEWHERE ON THE NORTH RUSSIAN FRONT.

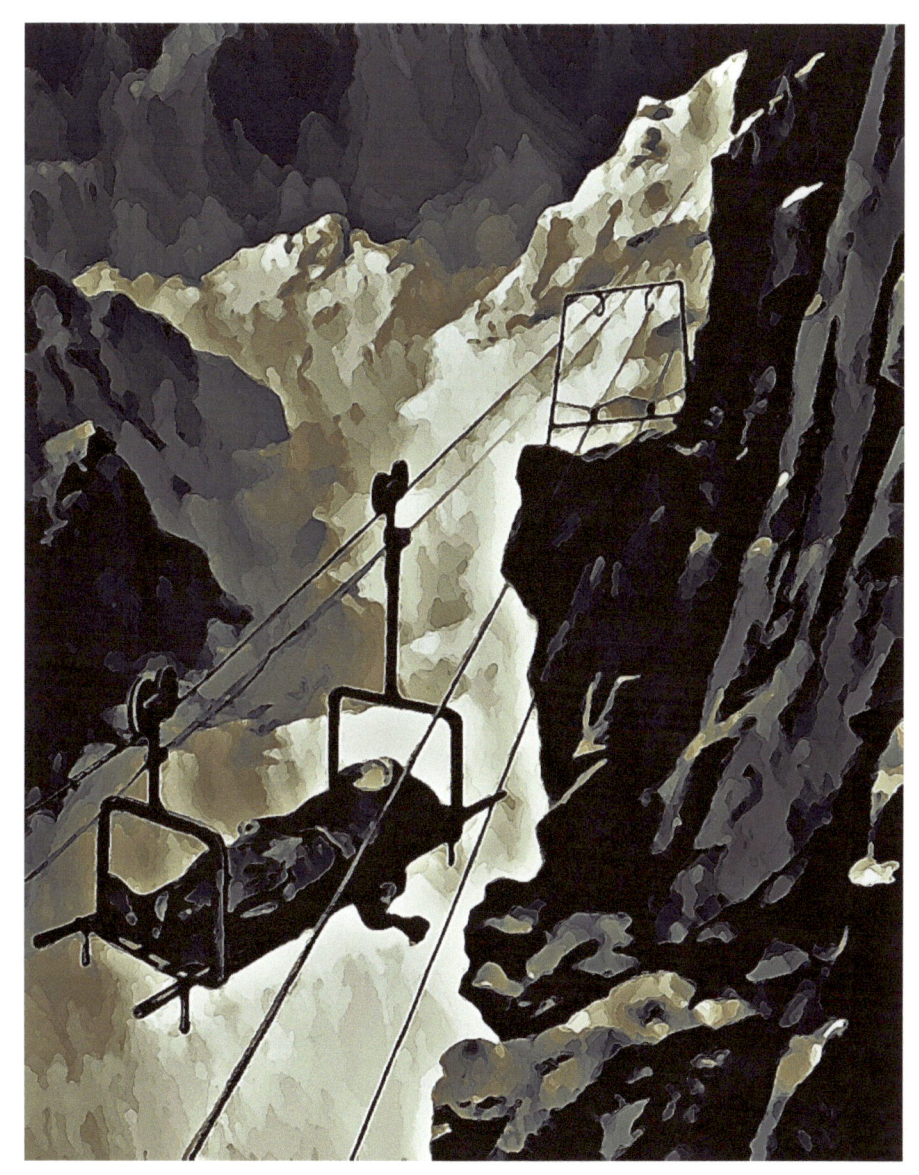

WOUNDED MEN RETURN BY WIRE THROUGH SPACE.

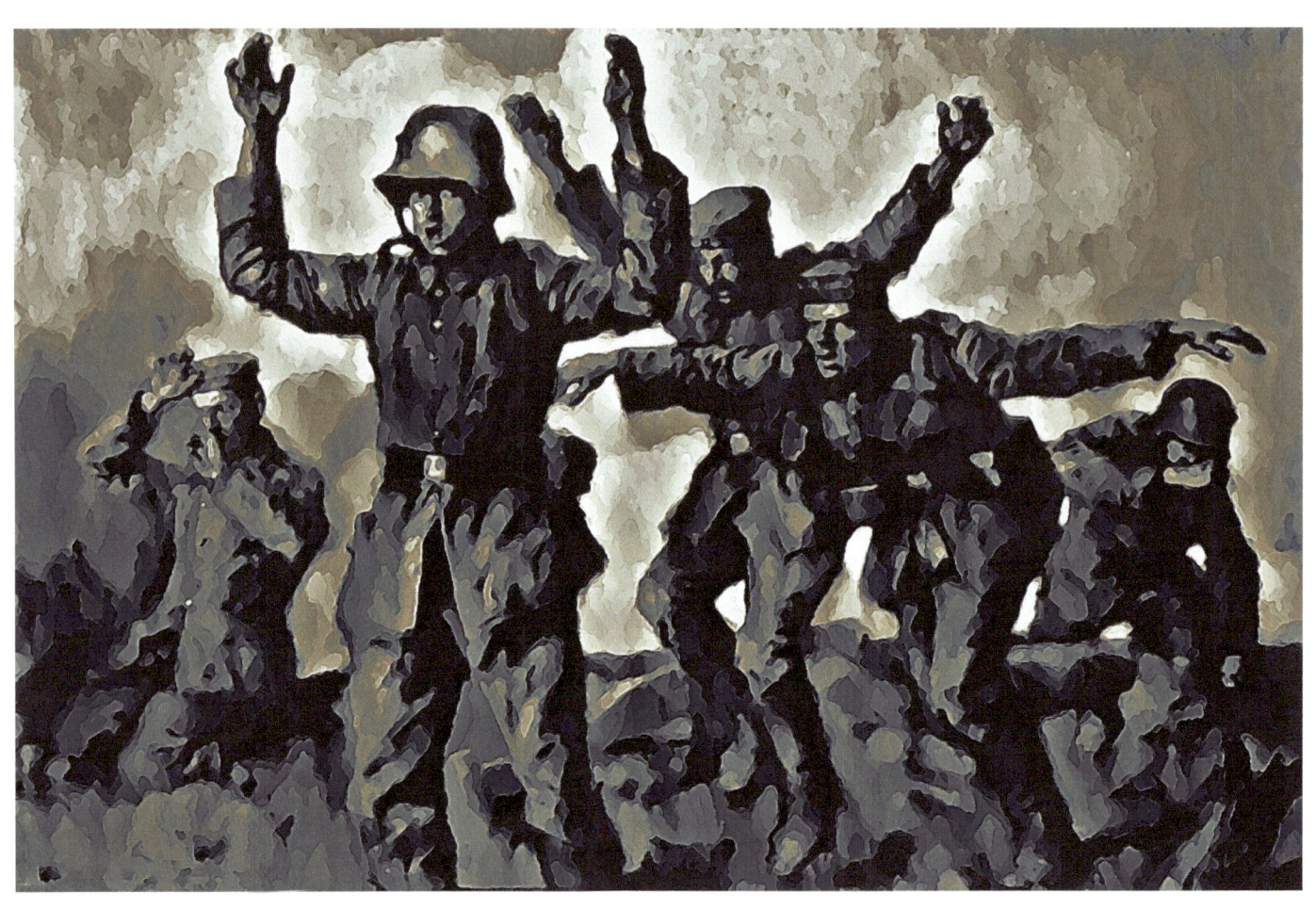

"KAMERAD! KAMERAD! PARDON!"

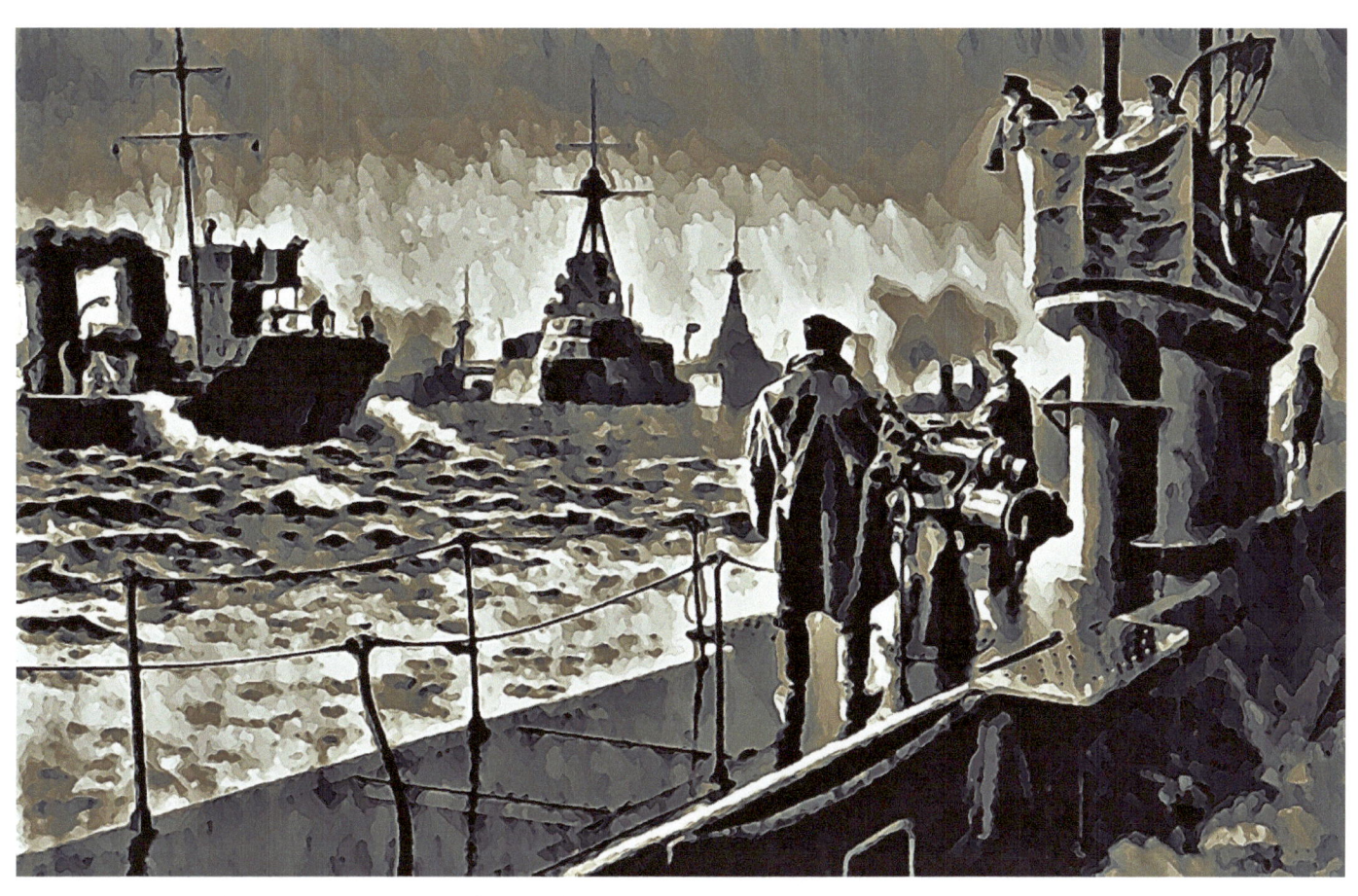
INCOMING DESTROYER (LEFT)) GREETING A BRITISH SUBMARINE GOING OUT ON PATROL DUTY.

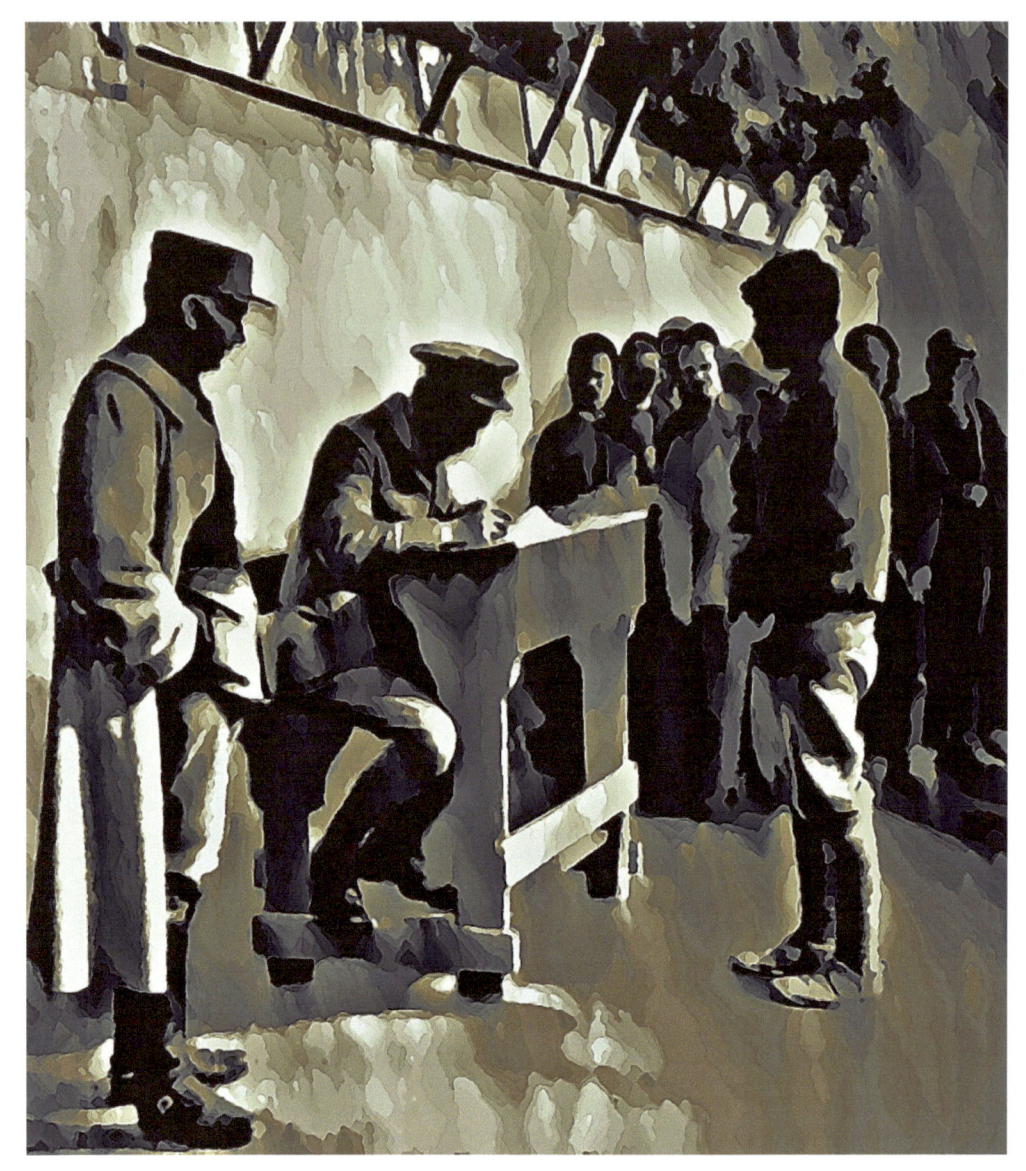
PERMITS FOR THE WAR ZONE.

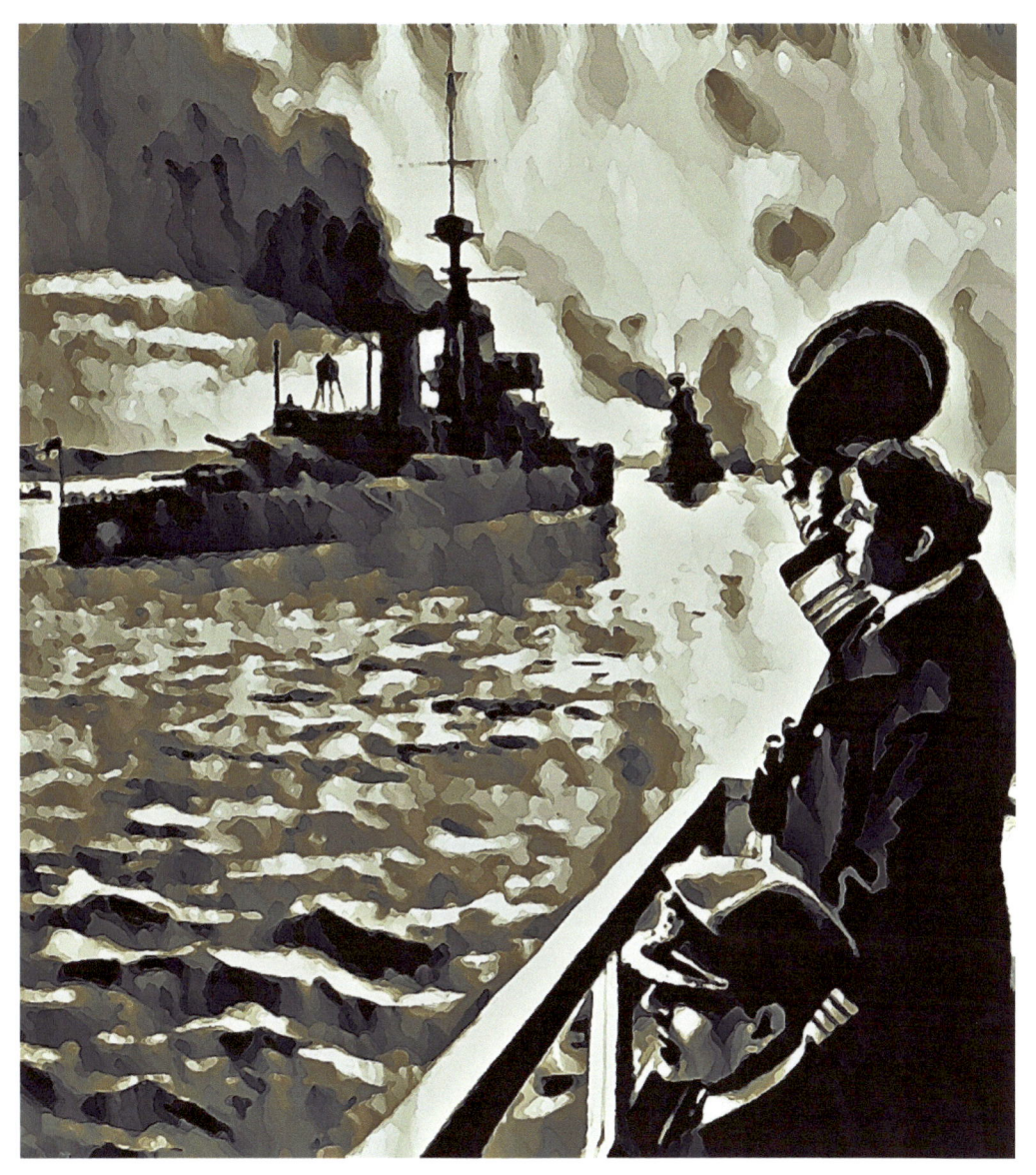

SUNSET ON GERMANY'S SEA-POWER.

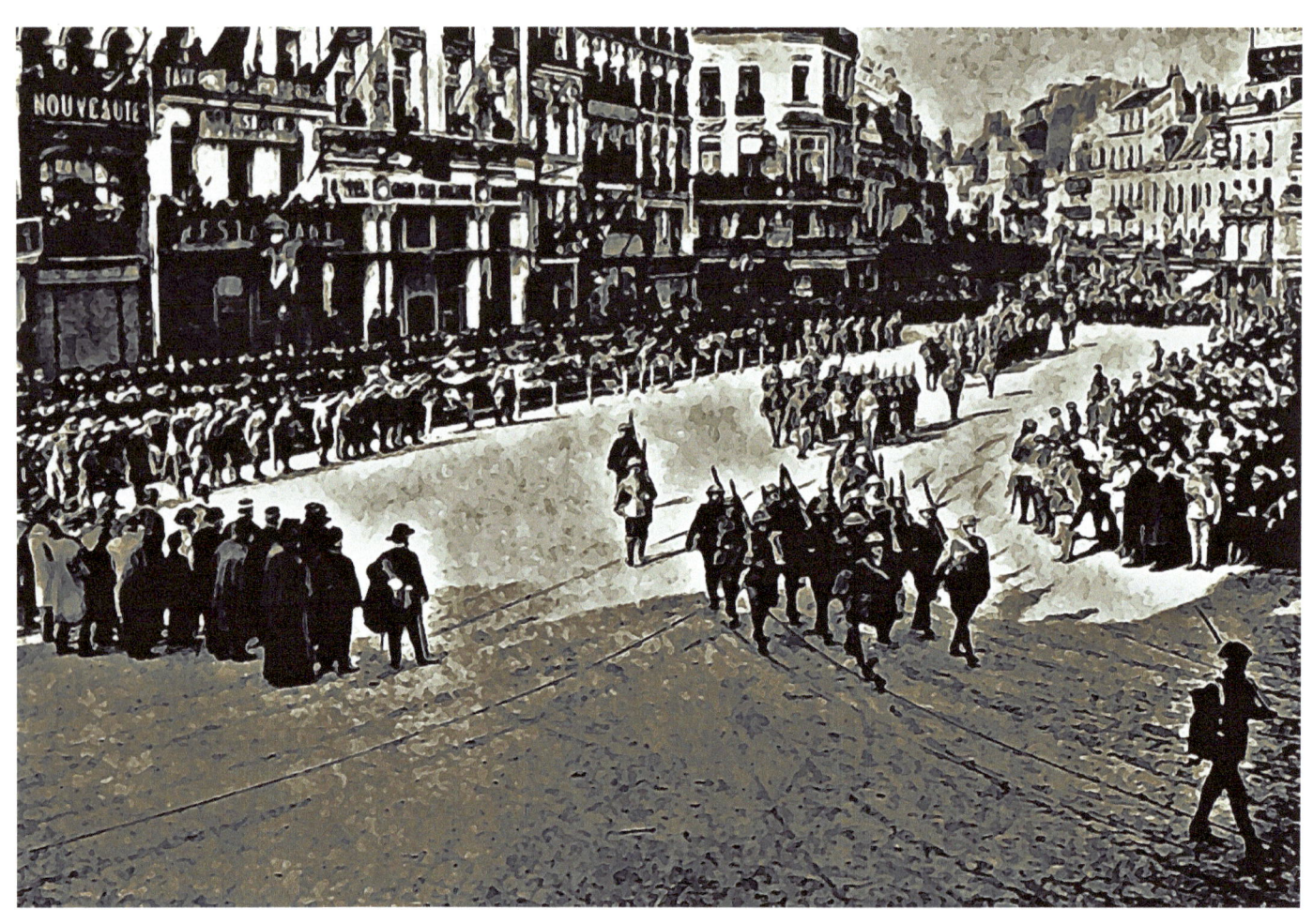

FORMAL ENTRY OF THE VICTORIOUS BRITISH FIFTH ARMY INTO LIBERATED LILLE, OCTOBER 28, 1918.

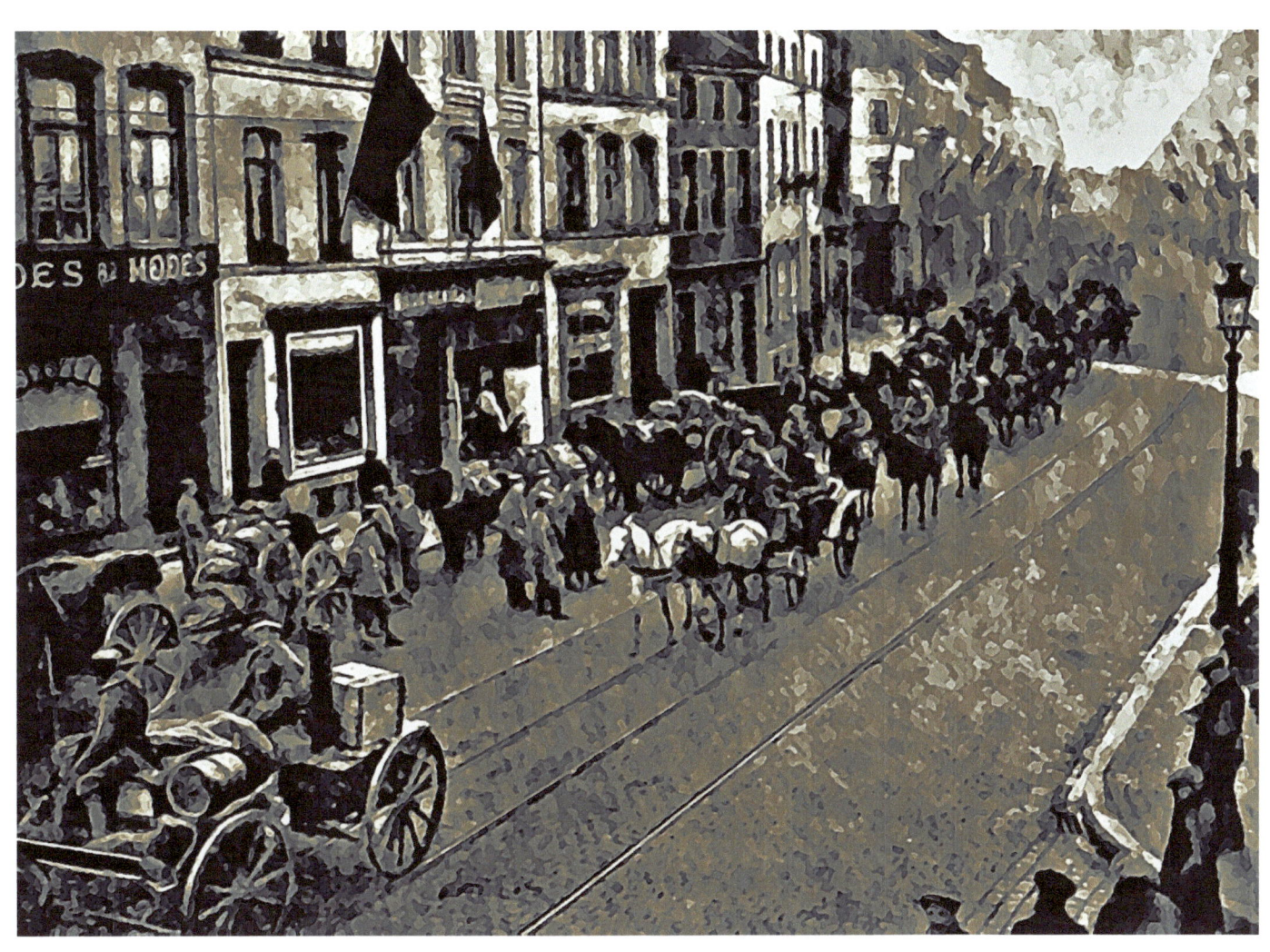

THE GERMAN EVACUATION OF BRUSSELS.

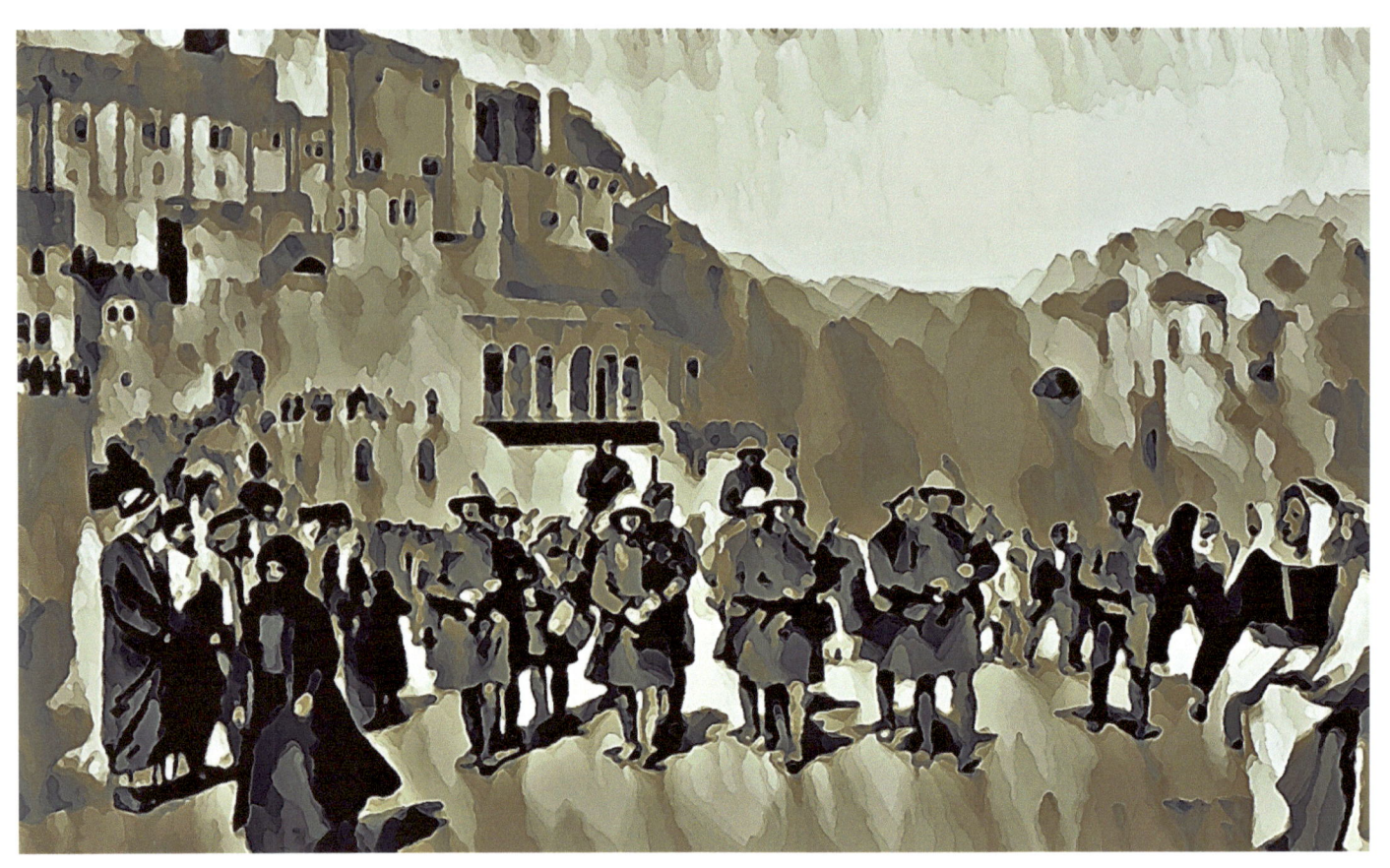

LONDON SCOTTISH MARCHING THROUGH ES SALT.

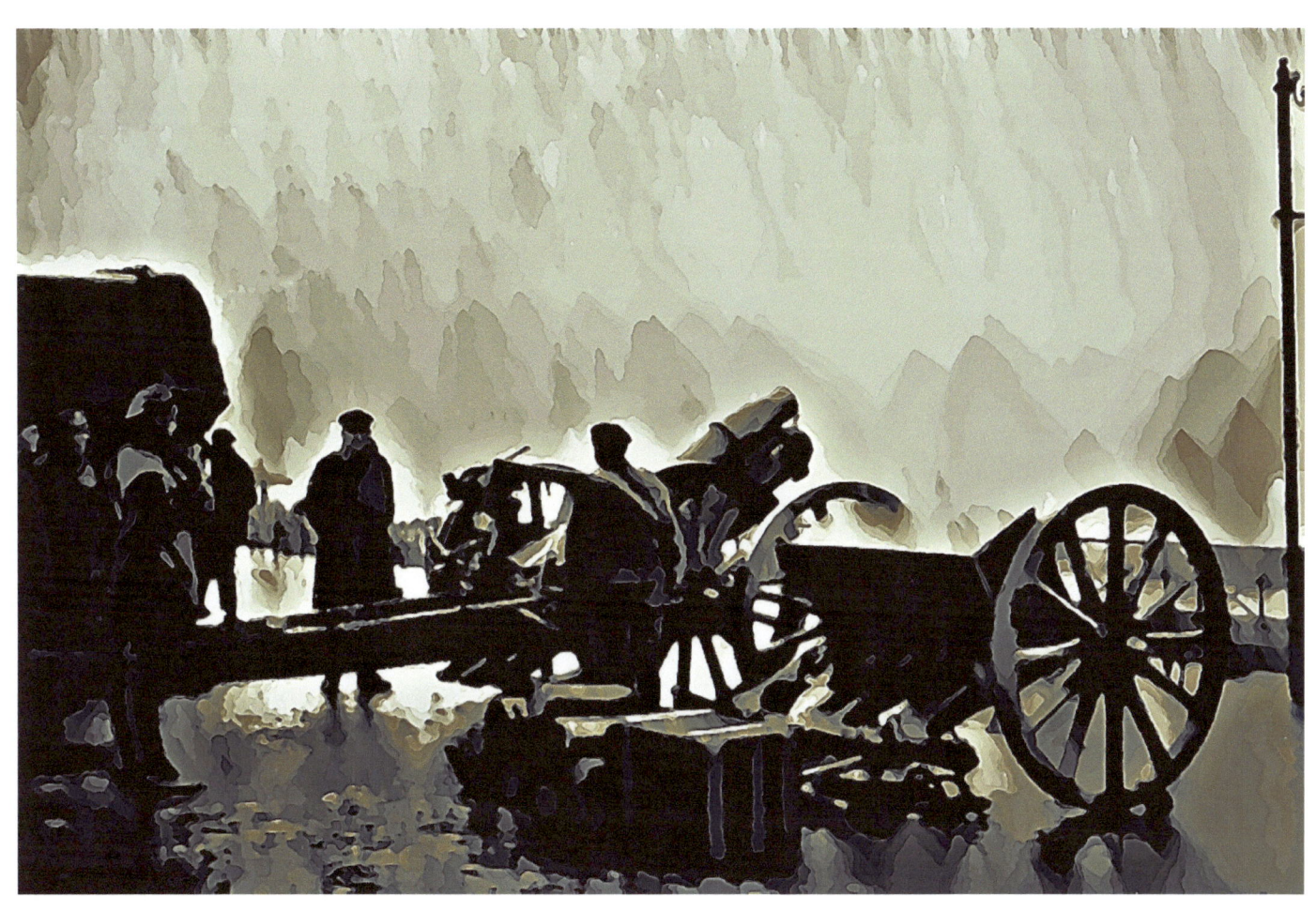
A BIG BRITISH HOWITZER AT COLOGNE, POINTING OVER THE RHINE.

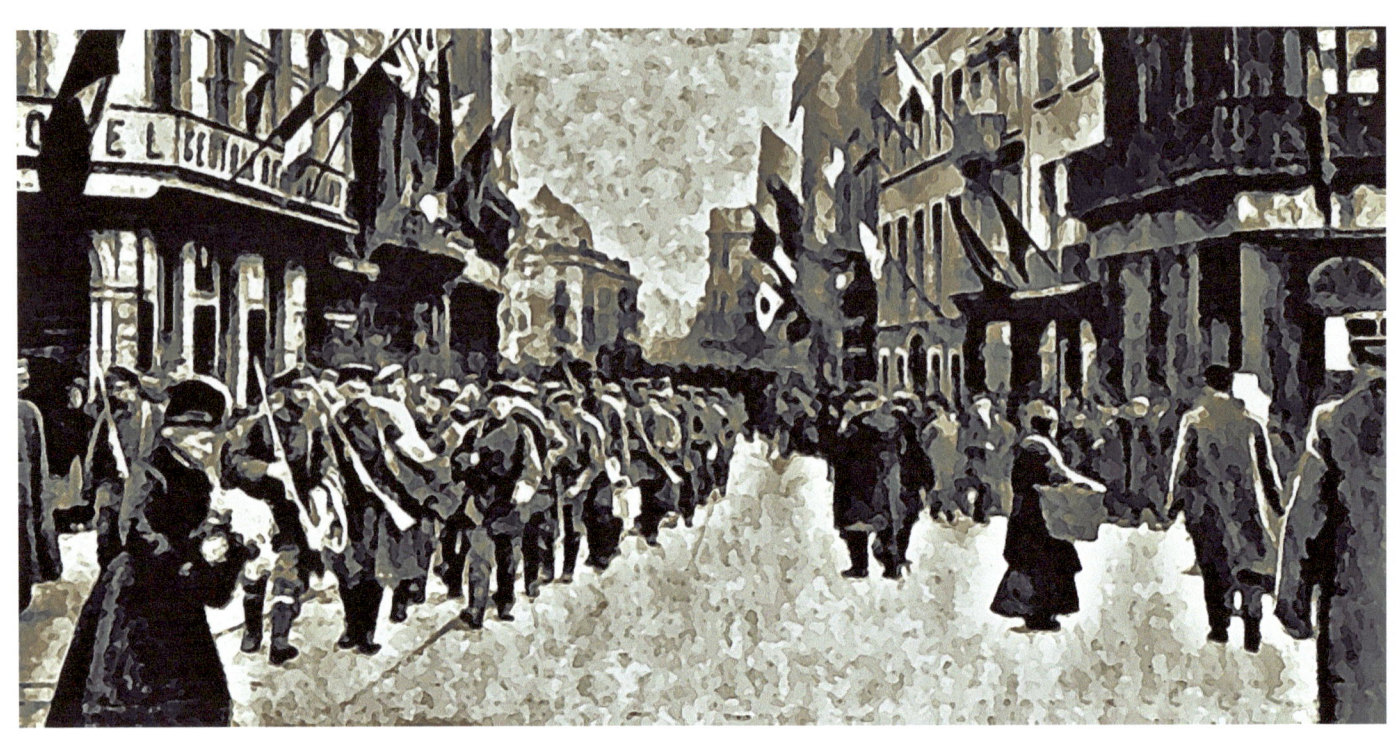

GERMAN TROOPS MARCHING OUT OF LIEGE.

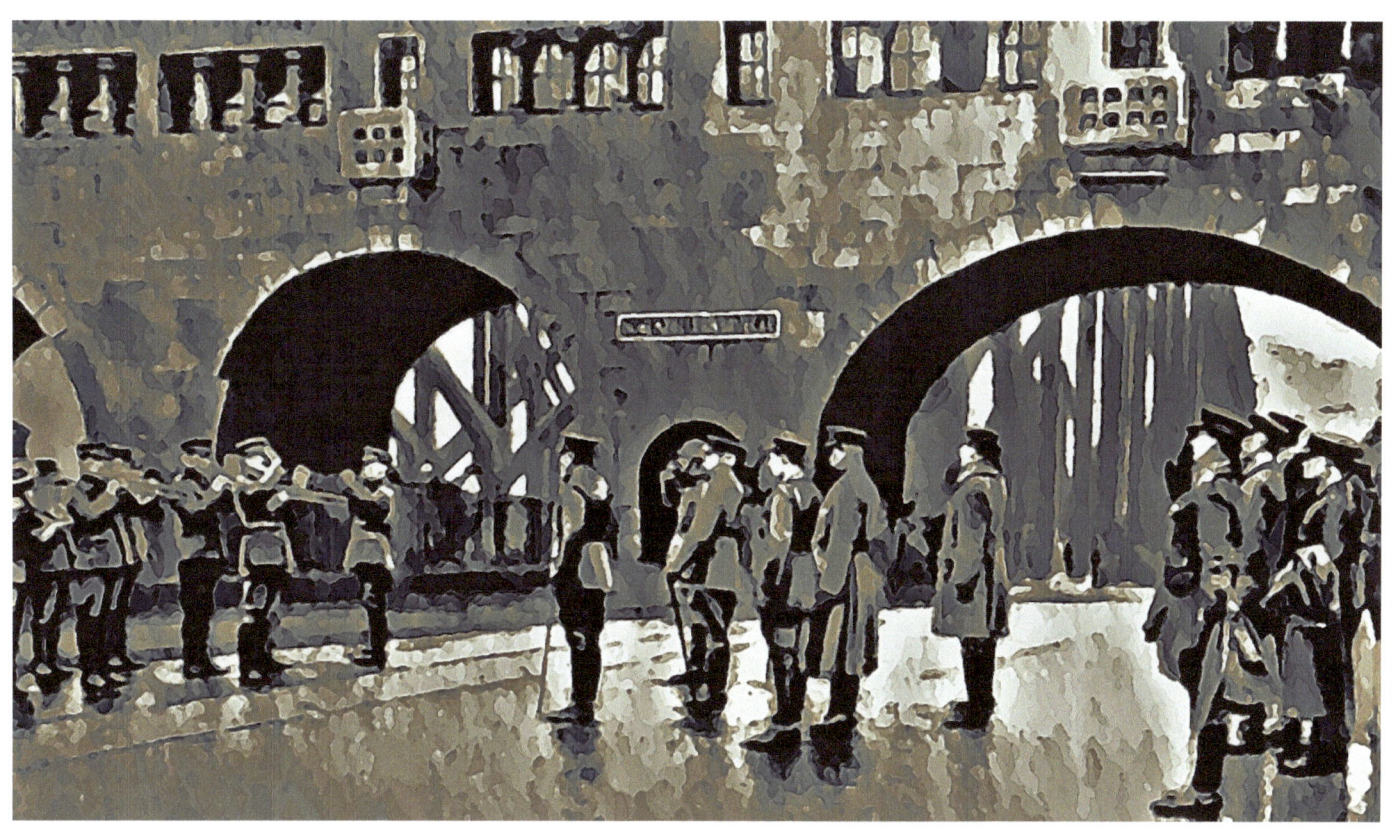

GENERAL PLUMER AND MEMBERS OF HIS STAFF STANDING AT THE SALUTE WHILE THE BAND PLAYED THE NATIONAL ANTHEM, BEFORE THE BRITISH TROOPS MARCHED ACROSS THE HOHENZOLLERN BRIDGE AT COLOGNE TO OCCUPY THE BRIDGE-HEAD ON THE EASTERN BANK.

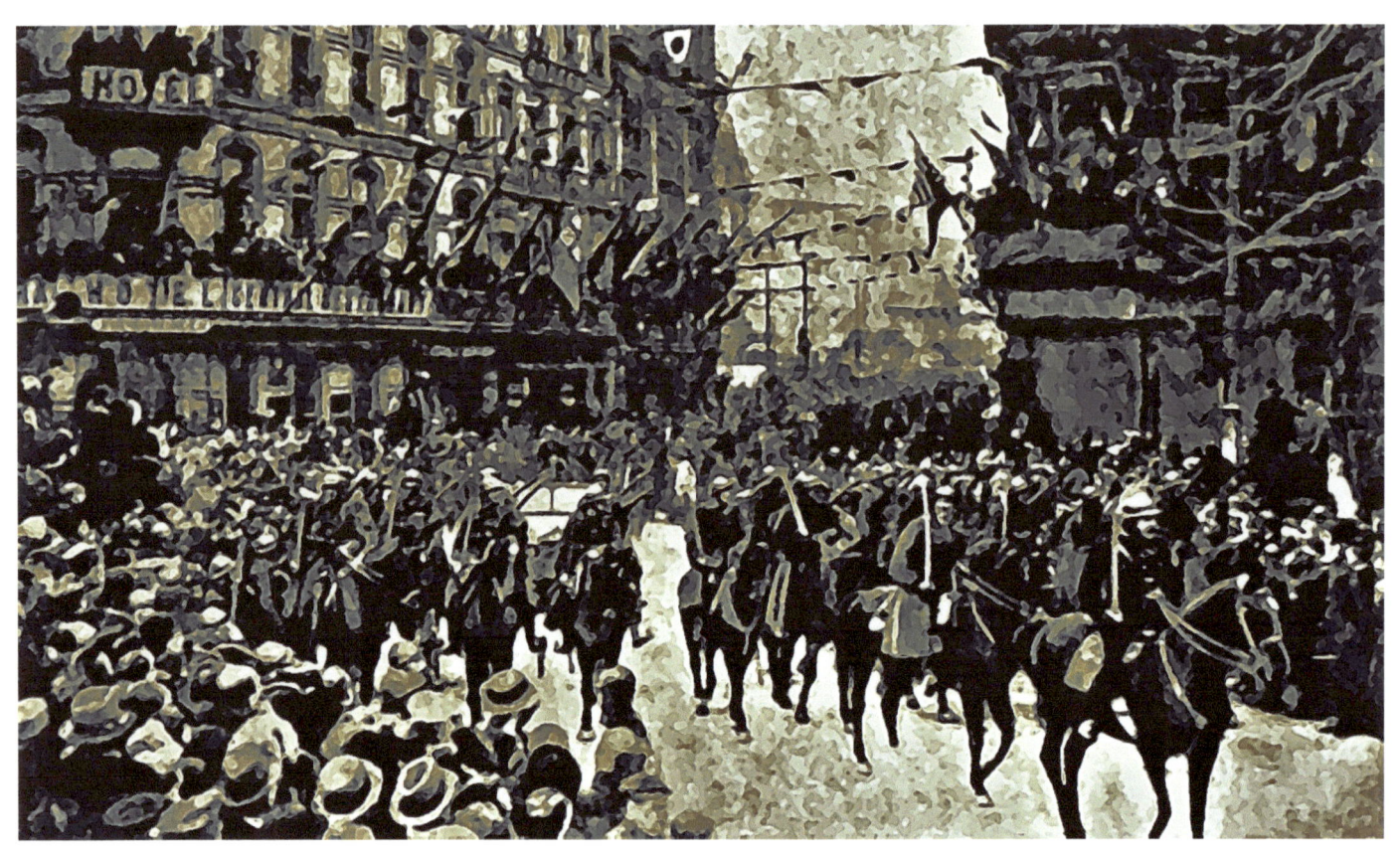

HEROIC LEIGE REOCCUPIED.

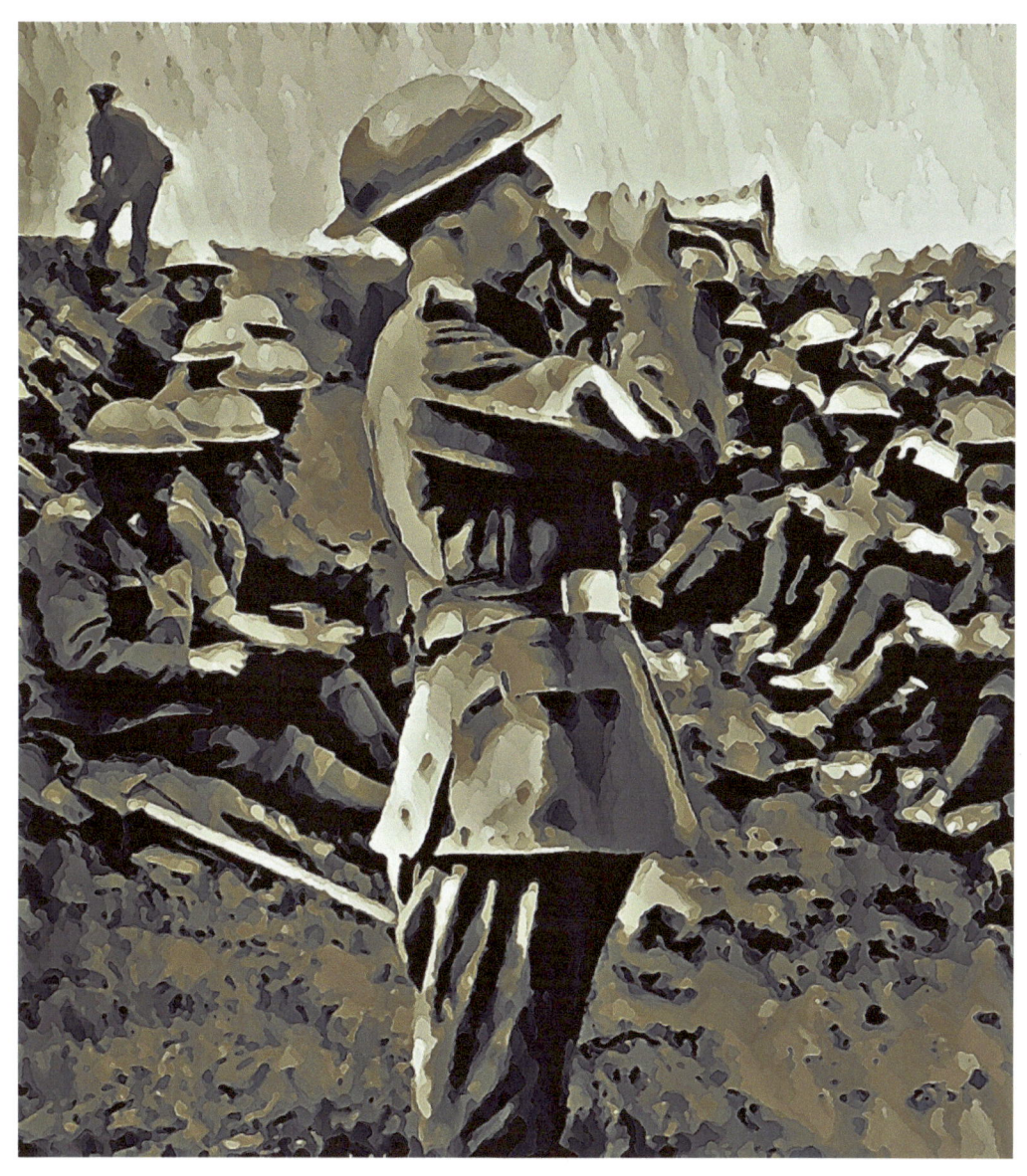
"CEASE FIRE!" 11 A.M., NOVEMBER 11, 1918.

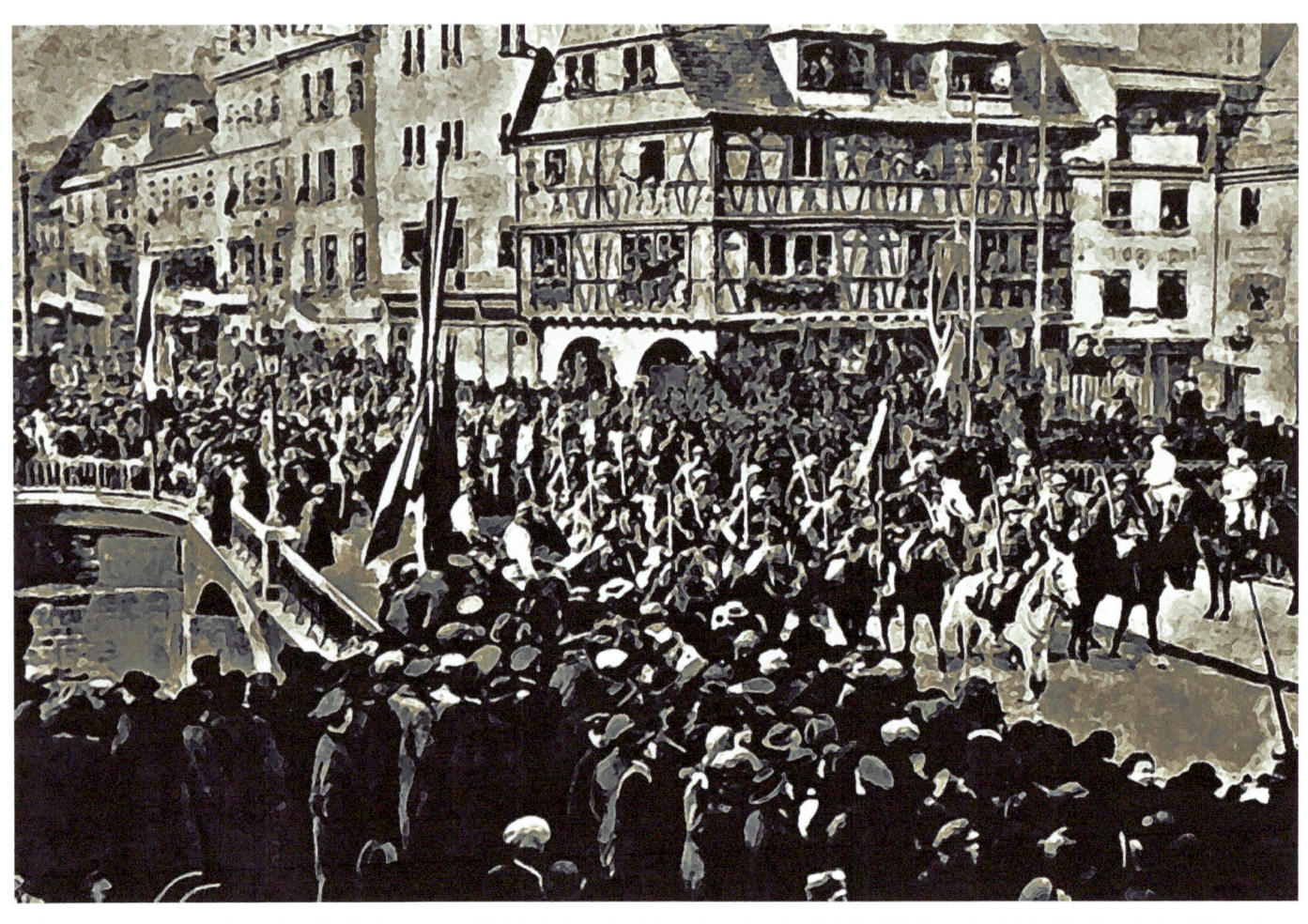

TRIUMPHANT ENTRY OF FRENCH CAVALRY INTO STRASBOURG, CAPITAL OF LIBERATED ALSACE, NOVEMBER, 1918.

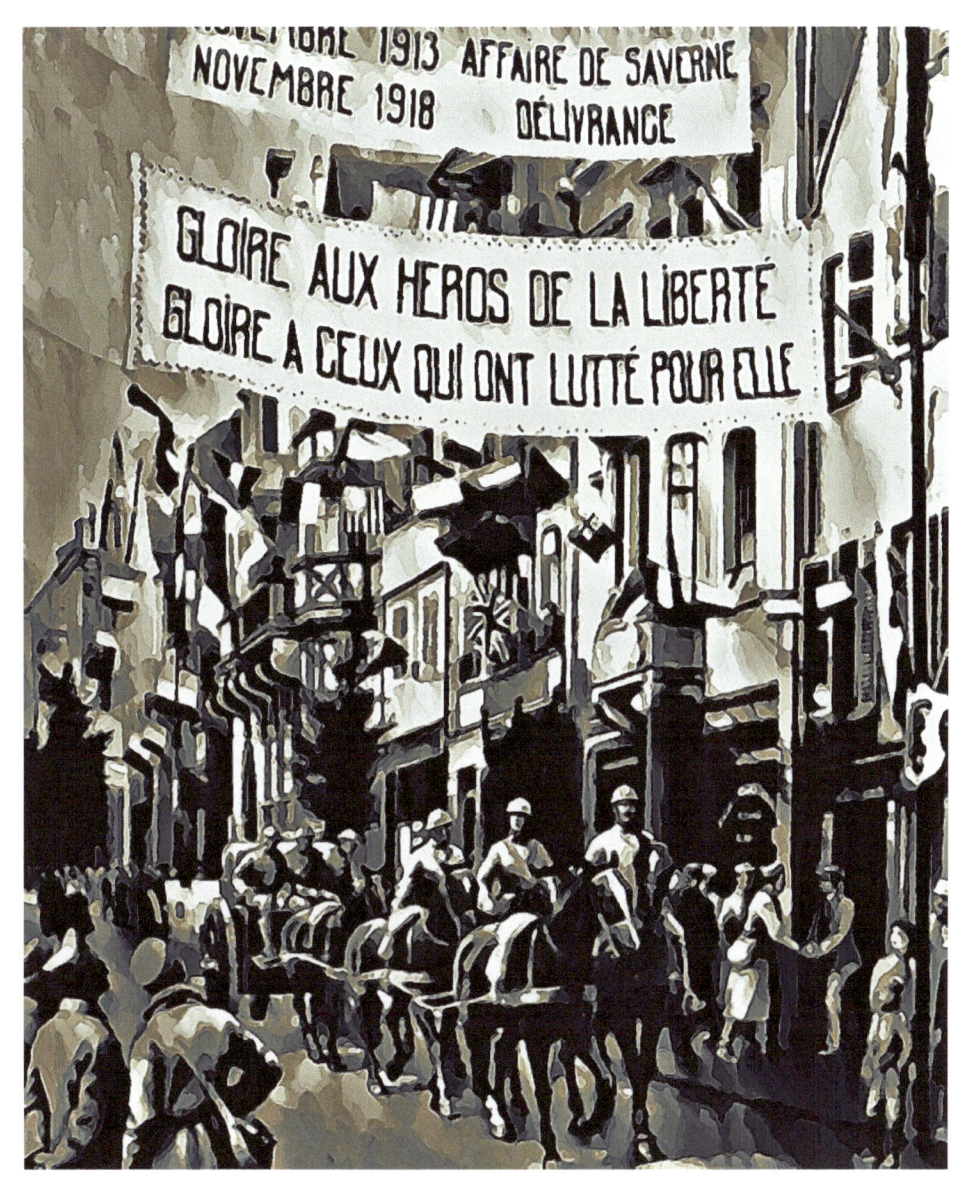

AFTER FIVE YEARS.

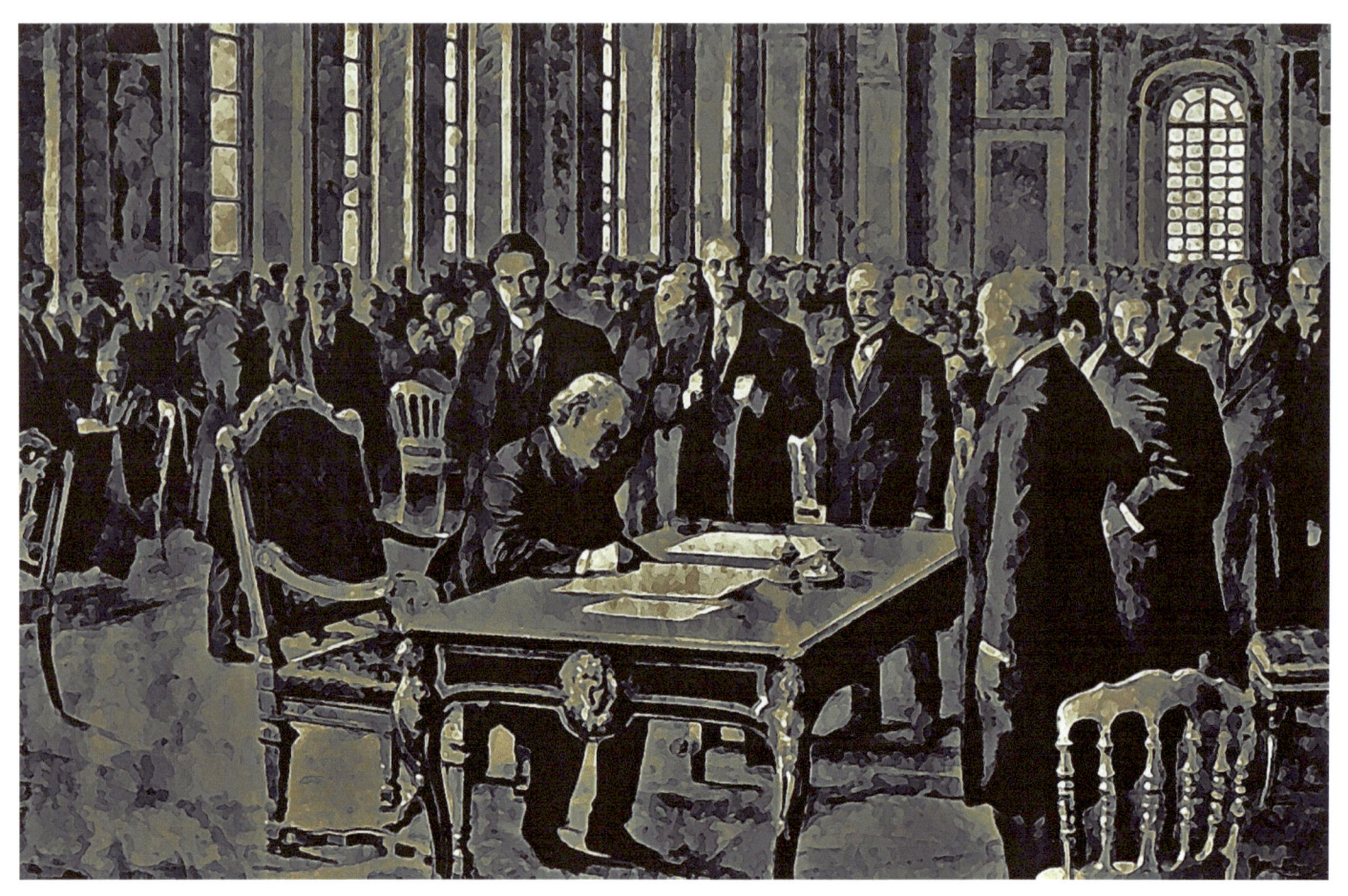
SIGNING THE PEACE TREATY.

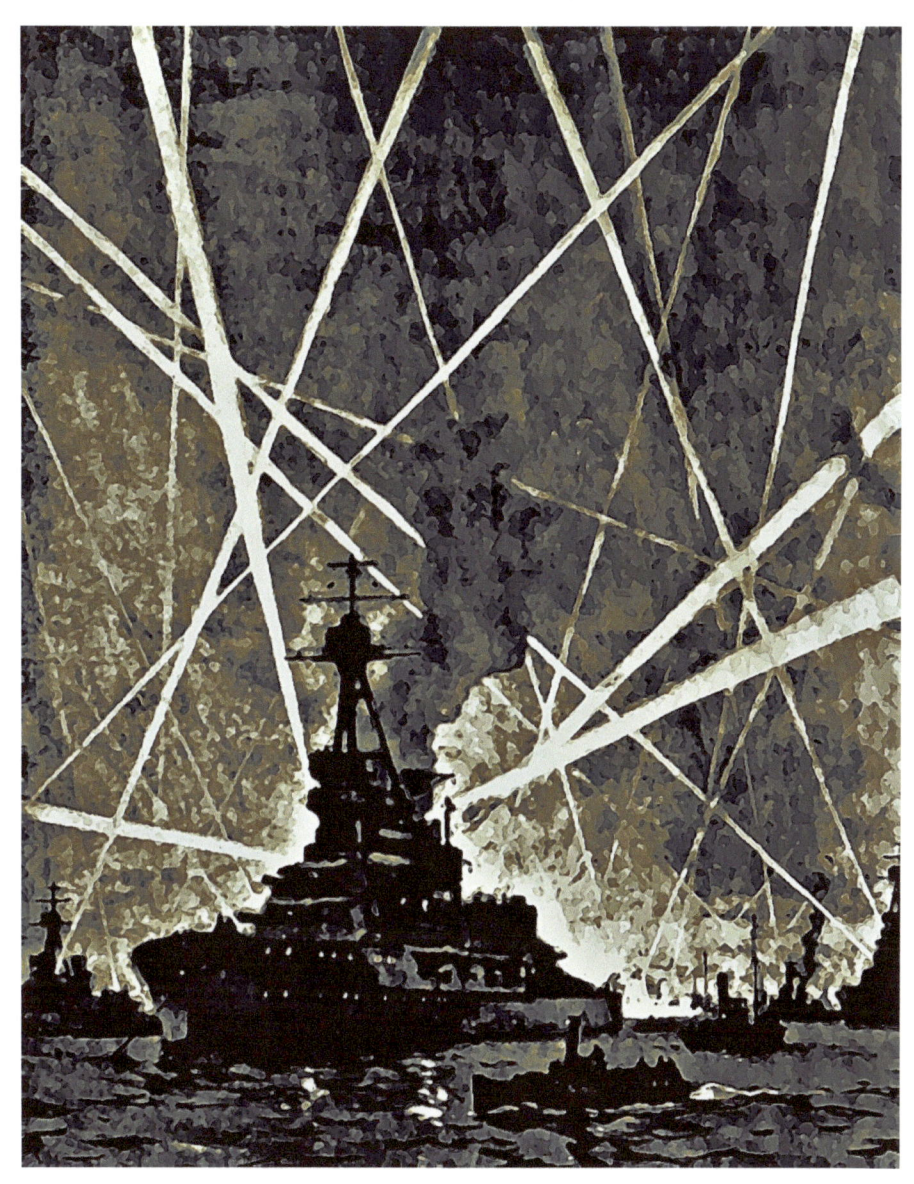
BRITISH NAVY CELEBRATING THE SIGNING OF THE ARMISTICE.

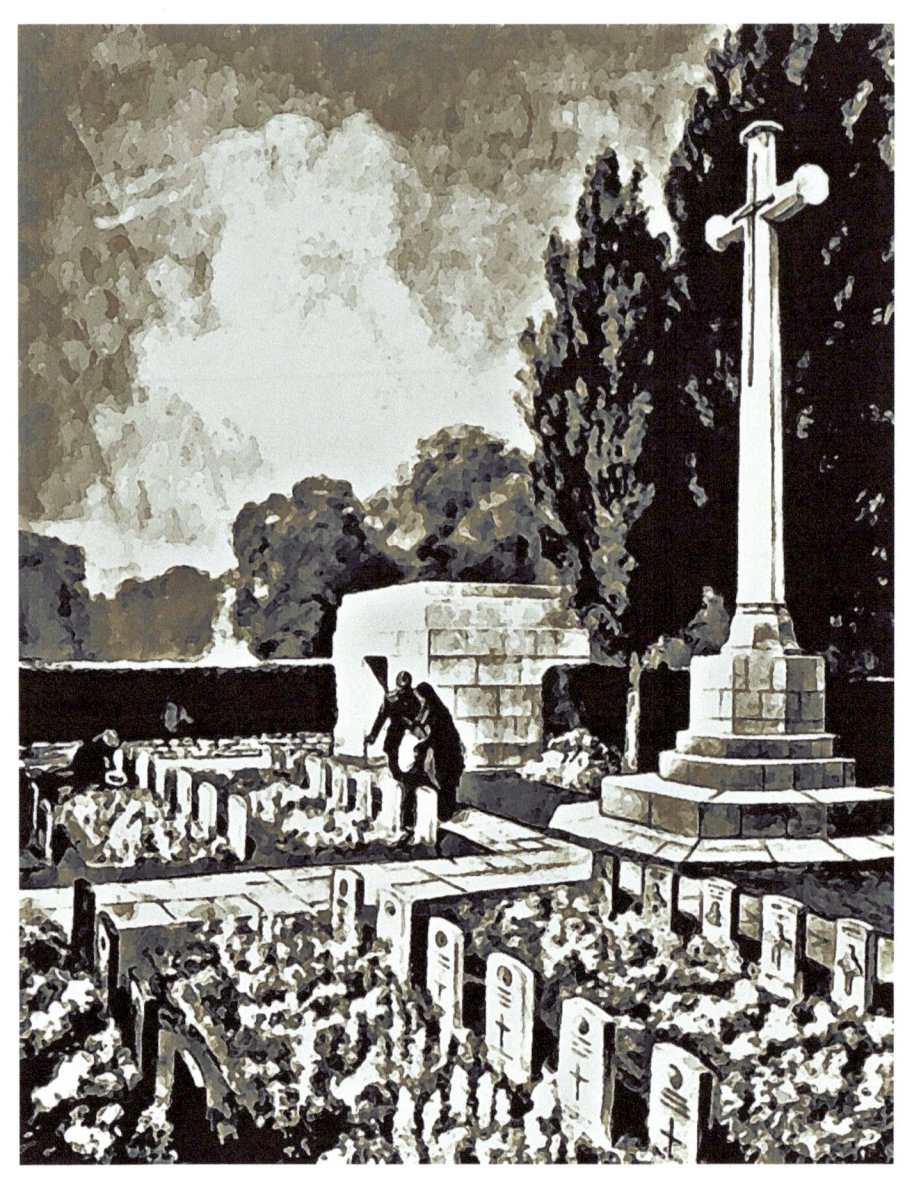
THE MEMORIAL CROSS OF SACRIFICE.

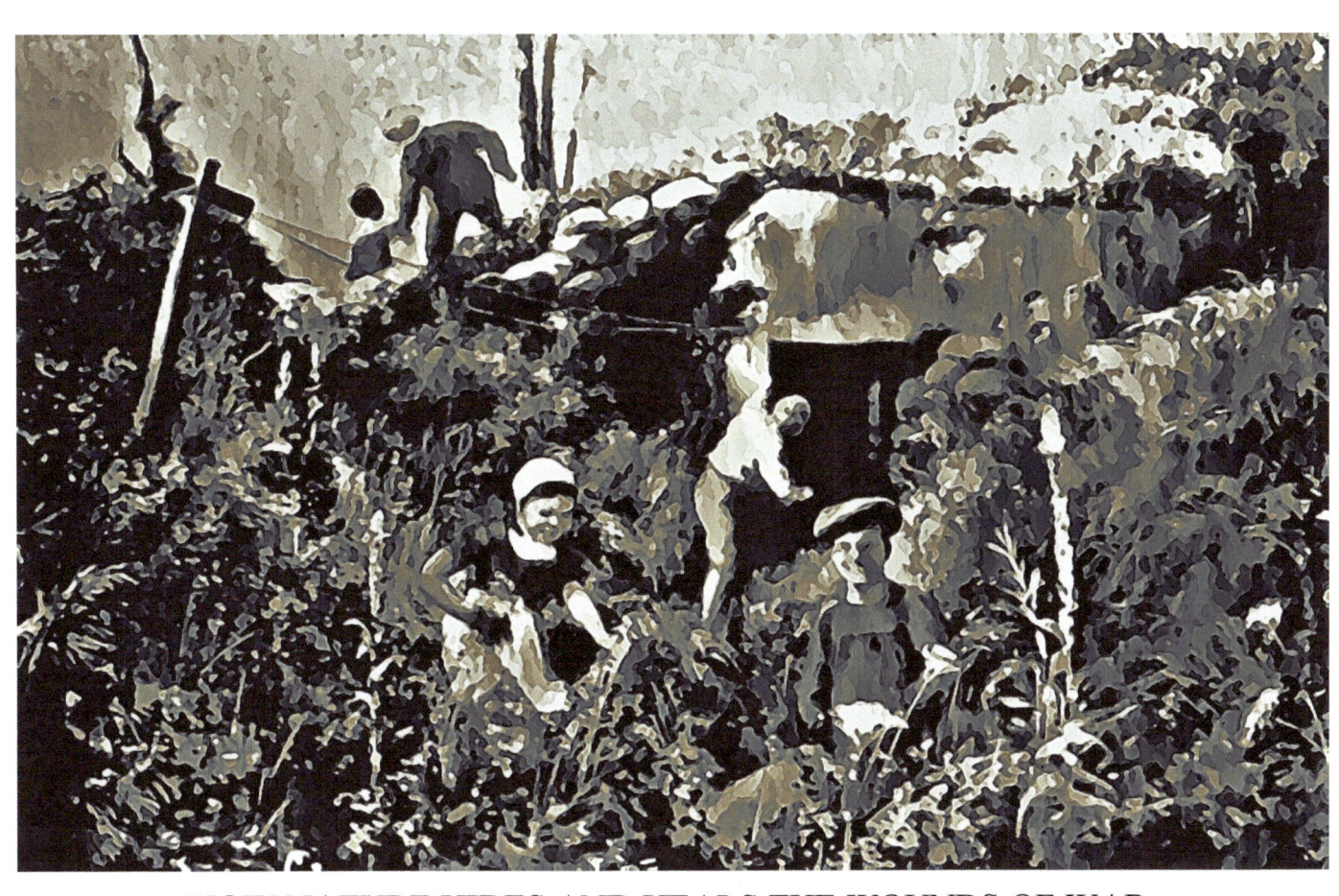
HOW NATURE HIDES AND HEALS THE WOUNDS OF WAR.

www.ingramcontent.com/pod-product-compliance
Lightning Source LLC
Chambersburg PA
CBHW040451220526
45473CB00004B/1599